INVENTORS

GUIDEBOOK

by
Melvin L. Fuller

edited by
Maggie Weisberg

Cartoons by Don Christensen

Glossary of Patent Terms and Usage
by Lawrence Fleming

iii

PUBLISHED IN THE
UNITED STATES OF AMERICA
BY

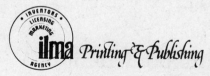

First Printing 1971
Second Printing 1973
Third Printing - Revised 1974
Fourth Printing 1975
Fifth Printing - Revised 1976
Sixth Printing 1978
Seventh Printing - Revised 1980
Eighth Printing - Revised 1984

ILMA PRINTING & PUBLISHING
P.O. Box 251
Tarzana, CA 91356
818/344-3375

Originally conceived and written by Melvin L. Fuller
Edited 1974 by Maggie Weisberg
Cartoons by Don Christensen
Glossary of Patent Terms & Usage by Larry Fleming

© Copyright ILMA Printing & Publishing 1984
ISBN 0-930317-30-0

DEDICATION

One of the greatest experiences of my life came with a cognition, i.e., a sudden realization, a knowingness that something needed to be done to bring order into the invention field and that I, personally, must assume the responsiblity to get it done. Since then, in spite of much discouragement, many delays and interference and disinterest from those who should be helping, but with dedicated and loving help from many more, what I set out to do has been well begun. We now have enough people in full agreement of our goals that the continuity of our efforts is assured.

This Handbook is only a guide, but in this current revision, I pass on the digested results of twelve years of effort and the introduction of the Teach Board in 1982, which has necessitated a major reorganization of the material contained herein.

My particular thanks to Louise, my uncomplaining wife, who permitted me the freedom, while performing the lackluster routine work of administration, and to my teammate and business partner, Maggie Weisberg, who has yet to find her "Level of Incompetence," according to the Peter Principle. Every new challenge causes her to expand. It is awesome to see, and one wonders where her limits are, if indeed she has any.

We have had a great deal of help from many Chapter Chairmen, some of whom served and then moved on to their own missions and others who still serve. The list of those who have made IWI successful grows each day, and space prohibits listing them all by name. But, my heartfelt thanks embraces all of them.

—Melvin L. Fuller

INTRODUCTION

This **Inventors Guidebook** by Melvin L. Fuller, has designed to provide, within the covers of one comprehensive volume, a most effective navigational tool with direct and practical answers to the inventor's questions and problems.

The information contained in this guidebook will be found to be specific and to the point. The excellent forms, tables, shortcuts, listings of facts, outlines of procedures—all of these will save the inventor immeasurable time, trouble, frustration and expense. Whether the problem to be dealt with relates to protection, disclosure documents, preliminary patent search, prototypes, contracts and agreements, trademarks and copyrights—to mention only a few of the subjects included—the Guidebook supplies the most reliable and latest information in the most concise form.

Because of the differences in background and areas of expertise of each inventor, and the nature and difference of each individual invention, no two inventors will be confronted with the same problems. Nevertheless, Melvin Fuller's innovative **Inventors Teach Board** will provide an inexhaustable source of informed, time-proven options for the inventor in the process of creating, developing, protecting, patenting, liscensing or manufacturing his or her product, all the way to marketing and sales.

Within this book will be found not only the "how-to" and "why", but a comprehensive bibliography, an excellent compilation of forms, and an invaluable glossary of pertinent and terms unique to the profession of inventing.
The ingenuity of the American inventor (so ably demonstrated by the author of this book), in successful collaboration with the effective American manufacturer, together constitute one of America's greatest assets and resources. Had the diverse and pertinent material embodied in this book been available to me when I obtained the first of some thirty patents that I hold, I would have been spared much loss of time, anguish and costs.

So, to all inventors who set out on the arduous but rewarding adventure of conceptualizing and bringing forth a new product or process, happy sailing. Your frail craft will be far more seaworthy with the trustworthy instruments provided in this guidebook. It is a challenging voyage, and there are no limits to how far you can go, or what shores you can reach.

—**Teri Pall, Ph.D.**

FOREWORD

The individual inventor is amazingly durable. Popularly typecast as an eccentric in earlier days - from the White Knights in "Alice" to Professor O.G. Wottasnozzle of comic strip fame during the '30s - he was re-typecast after World War II as a dead duck, supplanted by teams of anonymous scientists in white smocks who worked for hire in the prestigious Research and Development departments that began to proliferate in large corporations.

The new image grew. The annual American expenditure reported for industry R&D expanded from $160 million for the year 1930 to over $30 billion by the end of the '60s—an increase of some 200%.

There were official predictions of great technological progress, but nothing much happened to the rate of invention. Fifty-three thousand patents were issued in 1932; 50,000 in 1969; and in 1981, 65,865.

The early period from about 1900 to 1940 saw the general commercial introduction of cars, movies, home appliances, color printing, air conditioning, radio, sound recording, air transport and television. The decades since World War II have been far less progressive. Except for tape recording and computer technology, the innovations have run to atomic bombs, nuclear power, guided missiles and spacecraft. The public pays for such things collectively but for the most part doesn't reap direct benefits from them.

Large scale government and corporate spending on R&D has recently been declining. The costly experiment has not worked out. Some corporations are even admitting publicly that the output from such research and development has fallen short of expectations.

Through thick and thin the individual inventor has never stopped creating, and Inventors Workshop International hopes the decade of the '80s will see him finally coming into his own.

This book has been written toward that end — to help guide individual inventors to success. The text herein provides factual, realistic and basic guides to the processes involved — from dealing with patents and trademarks through negotiations with manufacturers and the starting up of a business. The information contained herein is based on the first-hand experience of those who work in these fields.

IMPORTANT NOTE

In reading this book be very certain you never read beyond a word you do not fully understand.

The only reason a person gives up a study or becomes confused or unable to learn is that he or she has not stopped to look up and make sure he fully understands each and every word.

If the material becomes confusing or difficult to grasp, you will find by back tracking that there is a word earlier that you have not understood. Don't read any further. Go back - find the misunderstood word and look up the definition in a good dictionary.

TABLE OF CONTENTS

TABLE OF CONTENTS

WHAT IS INVENTORS WORKSHOP INTERNATIONAL EDUCATION FOUNDATION ALL ABOUT?

*I*nventors Workshop International Education Foundation is a dynamic, nonprofit membership organization born out of the need for protection for those men and women - the individual inventors of this world - whose creativity has given us just about everything we use in our everyday lives. Melvin L. Fuller, the founder and president of the Workshop, is himself an inventor who through personal experience, became aware of the desperate need for an ethical organization to which inventors could turn for help. He had seen great ideas lost for lack of proper protection and others flounder for lack of procedural know-how. He had seen inventors fleeced by unscrupulous promoters, and sometimes even our laws seem inimical to the interests of the inventor.

IWI seeks to provide a haven from the predatory and unethical practices employed so prevalently in the invention "promotion" business. Although powerless to halt this outragous exploitation of inventors, IWI can equip as many as will listen with the means of protecting themselves.

To this day it is common practice in many large companies to pay an employee $1.00 for an invention. The company is then at liberty to use the invention or kill it, and the inventor has lost forever his right to his own idea. The public also loses whatever benefit might have been derived from that ideas. This is patently unfair and the practice must not be permitted to continue.

The inventor creates jobs and wealth, improves the environment, fills social needs and builds a healthy economy. He is a special kind of person with a special kind of talent, and he plays an indispensable role in the advancement of human society. He needs special protection and ecouragement, and he has not been getting either from big business or government.

The individual inventor has always played a lone role. He can no longer afford to do so. He must unite with others who share his creative talent and make the inventor's voice a power to be reckoned with. In the past it has been business that has used its clout to get laws enacted in its favor. Inventors must do the same thing. In union there is strength. Only by working together can we bring about miracles.

The Workshop has struggled to maintain itself independent of outside control by avoiding grants and funding through foundations or government sources. IWI is financed by and is responsible solely to its members.

The Articles of the Workshop reflect its resolve:

"To secure for its members and associates just and equitable remuneration and reward for their genius, labor and efforts arising from or in connection with their inventions and discoveries, and to otherwise guide its members in the protection of such inventions and discoveries..."

2

IWI has been working several areas in furtherance of these goals, letting its views be known in Congress and taking up the banner whenever injustice is done to an Inventor, enhancing the Inventor's image, smoothing the path of inventions, and building membership numbers so that its words carry weight and the wishes of the Inventor are accorded attention and respect. The steady growth of the Workshop has resulted in the formation of several self-governing Chapters serving geographical areas. All that is needed to begin a local Chapter is a number of Inventors who recognize the powerful advantages of group action.

An affiliate organization — Inventors Licensing and Marketing Agency (ILMA) - has been formed to help member inventors sell or license their products. And from ILMA still other service organizations have sprouted to fill the needs of the individual inventor.

Inventors, poets and creative people in general have always been the harbingers of change. They have been — and are — the idealists and the doers -one step ahead of their fellow man. It will be up to them to create the better world of tomorrow.

There isn't an area of our lives that cannot be improved. The horizons are limitless, and the very survival of the world depends on some better answers. It is the inventor who will have to come up with them.

INVENTORS GUIDEBOOK
AND
INVENTORS TEACH BOARD

*T*he Inventors Guidebook and Inventors Teach Board have been prepared to aid and abet . . . to encourage and prod inventors to stir themselves and develop their ideas to the point of usability.

Set forth in this Guidebook and Teach Board in simple terms is a step-by-step program to help the Inventor take his idea through the various stages of protection, development, manufacturing and, finally, marketing. It is a major revision of the original Handbook, reflecting IWI's evolution in methodology brought about by 12 years of working with thousands of inventors in the protection and marketing of their inventions, creations and produced items. Use of the time-tested instructions in this Guidebook can save the Inventor thousands of dollars and countless hours of wasted motion during the process of making his product market ready.

The progressive steps, if followed with understanding, will assure that the Inventor will arrive successfully at the marketplace.

Once you are convinced of the worth of your ideas, don't pause or hesitate. Take it up these Steps until you reach completion - and success.

The Teach Board is a logic chain that incorporates, on an overview level, the important elements of taking an invention - and other forms of saleable creativity - from mind to market. and to learn and appreciate the interrelationship of the elements.

The Teach Board is the result of three years of evolution of the interaction of its elements, starting with a logic flow diagram and evolving into a gamelike approach. After all, inventing is a game - a game which has its rules, freedoms, barriers, risks, luck and winners and losers.

5

A brief examinantion of the Teach Board reveals that there are color groupings and a general progression from left to right and top to bottom. Board positions 1 through 9 deal with the subject of preliminary protection. Section I of the text of the Guidebook expands on the subject. Board positions 10 through 16 and Section II deal with patent protection and some of the elements of decision that enter into applying for patent, and what results to expect. The board and book complement each other and meld the many elements of inventing.

Is is an orderly progression and although their order is not fixed, and following them might not guarantee that you will make a million on your invention, it will improve your chances a hundredfold. You cannot sell something that is locked inside your head.

As with any journey, the biggest and most important step is the first one. Here it is. Take it.

Conception

The "flash of creative genius" is an almost mystical cognition that can apparently occur to several people in different parts of the world at the same time.

Narinder S. Kapany of the Department of Physics, Stanford University, Stanford, said in a speech he delivered to the Conference on the Public Need and Role of the Inventor in Monterey, California, June 1973:

"The act of inventing can be subconscious. I don't know how many inventors have invented in sleep, but I have. I recall one fine morning I got up and remembered that while I was at least half asleep I had thought of a method for measuring the refractive index of liquids photometrically. The idea is simple. You shine light into a glass rod, and when you inbed it into liquid to be tested, the critical angle for total reflection changes and, therefore, the amount of light transmitted through the rod changes. A photo detector placed at the other end of the rod thus measures the refractive index of the surrounding liquid. The irony of this mechanism of the inventive process is that maybe a lot of us invent during sleep and don't remember it the next morning."

Inventors have been known to lose all rights to their invention because they failed to make a record of the date the idea came to them. So it is very important to establish date of conception when you get that flash of genius...that moment when you know you have something new, novel and potentially valuable.

Documentation must establish date of conception, reduction to practice and diligence in writing, with qualified witnesses signing.

SECTION I

AN OVERVIEW

There are eight key steps that must be taken in order to get your idea off the ground — or out of your head — and to the marketplace. To complete the steps properly will take time, thought and care. None of the steps can be rushed . . . none can be omitted.

It is an orderly progression and although their order is not fixed, and following them might not guarantee that you will make a million on your invention, it will improve your chances a hundredfold. You cannot sell something that is locked inside your head.

As with any journey, the biggest and most important step is the first one. Here it is. Take it.

STEP 1—Protection

Patent Application

The Patent Application is the first thing that is thought of in connection with a new invention, and is the least logical step to take when conception first occurs. Notice that it doesn't appear on the Teach Board until position 17, and that there are vital itermediate steps in between.

At this point the form and function of the item have not been thought invention. First there must be drawings, test models and other works. Patent action is a premature expense when an idea is only half developed. One must first determine that the idea is worth the investment of money and time.

DOCUMENTATION

These are several paths of action open at the moment of conception. You can have a patent attorney or agent institute a patent application, OR you can comply with the Patent Office Disclosure Document Program, OR you can complete the Date of Conception Document described in this step.

Let's examine these alternatives.

9

Documentation is required to make tangible the abstract intellectual property, which as the word implies are intangible ideas and concepts - real only in the universe of the creator. To make it real in the physical universe, it must be agreed to by others. This is done by witnesses who document their understanding of the reality. Legally the description, if adequately formal, as in a patent application, is considered reduction to practice, even though a physical model hasn't been produced.

Documentation comes in several forms. They are all discussed below. They are NOT all recommended. Recommended is the Inventors Journal and, when and if ready, a Patent Application. Also, a Trademark should be registered as soon as the product is made and sold interstate, and a Copyright should be used wherever it applies. NOT recommended is the Date of Conception Document — not because it isn't a valid document, but because it is unnecessary if you are properly maintaining an Inventors Journal. The same thing applies to the Disclosure Document Program; it too, is a wasted $10 if you are keeping your Inventors Journal. But let us examine each document so that there are no misunderstandings.

Date of Conception Document

Describing your invention on the Date of Conception Document is easier if you start by saying, "My Invention is...." You might continue with, "a design..." or "a machine..." followed by an explanation of what your invention will do. Remember, it is not the purpose of the Date of Conception Document to produce drawings and details. All that is done later in the Journal or on the Patent Application. You have just conceived the idea, and its development will evolve through several models, drawings and studies.

Get the form witnessed by two people who are competent to understand the disclosure and who are not related to you.

Sign the form in the presence of a Notary Public who will attest that you are the person who signed the Date of Conception Document. His seal will be your proof that you conceived this invention at a date no later than the date of the notarization. It is not necessary for the notary to witness the signatures of the witnesses who attested to the Conception Document.

Have a photocopy made of the form - Notary Seal and all - and file the original with your important record.

Be sure to record the Date of Conception Document in your Inventor's Journal.

Senate Bill 683 was introduced in 1971 to revise the Title 35 Patent Law. It contained the following sentence as a condition of patentability:
"One year of inactivity with respect to the invention shall prima facia constitute abandonment."

This thought was carried forward as a "year of grace" in Senate Bill 1321, which was a 1973 revision of the 1971 S683. There are many other interesting proposals in consideration at the time of this writing, most of which are not to the advantage of the individual non-professional inventor.

It is recommended that all inventors avail themselves of currently proposed legislation by writing to their Senator or Congressman. On very rare occasions an idea is salable without further development. But when an idea is exposed, it can be lost, unless great care is taken in documenting all the circumstances. This step, Date of Conception, applies equally to the intangible idea. Usually a great deal of work must be done to "sell" an idea. More often it is the work itself which is most valuable and protectable.

We suggest that another way is to brainstorm your idea. Put your idea down on paper, and then list all the things you know about it. Good ideas and inventions are not developed overnight. Once you have done this and distilled your idea, put it aside... let it cool off.

At this point, let your subconscious take over. Einstein used this method to solve many of his great mathematical equations. After he had fed all facets of a problem into his subconscious he would take a walk, play the violin and let the problem simmer - until suddenly the subconscious spewed out the answer like a computer.

Now start improving and analyzing. Is your idea practical? Will it create other problems that will make its use impractical?

One of the Workshop members invented a product that seemed to be a winner. It was a swinging bar over the swimming pool. It was inexpensive, easy to install, and it filled a very definite need. It was used with much enjoyment by the inventor's family in their swimming pool, and when it was offered to the market it met with much enthusiasm. The manufacturer, however, rejected it because of possible liability and danger of user injury. The inventor is now looking for another use for a rigid 2" pipe.

Product liability is the manufacturer's burden, and it has hit new products very hard with the advent of OSHA (Occupational Safety and Health Agency). So be practical.

Break the device down into its parts (mentally) and ask, "How many different ways can each of these things be done?" Find several and pick the best.

STEP 2—The Disclosure Document Program

As stated earlier, this program is unnecessary IF YOU ARE PROPER-LY MAINTAINING YOUR INVENTORS JOURNAL. The information provided in this Section is to permit you to examine, in detail, what the program is, so that you'll have no misunderstanding about it. You shouldn't fall for the con man's proposal to prepare this document for you for a fee. The front "phonies" have been known to charge as much as $150 to submit this document on someone's behalf.

Under this program the Patent Office accepts and preserves, for a period of two years, papers referred to as "Disclosure Documents." These papers may be used as evidence of the dates of conception of inventions.

The Program

A paper disclosing an invention and signed by the inventor or inventors may be forwarded to the Patent Office by the inventor (or by any one of the inventors when there are joint inventors), by the owner of the invention, or by the attorney or agent of the inventor(s) or owner. It will be retained for two years and then destroyed unless it is referred to in a separate letter in a related patent application within said two years.

A Disclosure Document is not a patent application, and the date of its receipt in the Patent Office will not become the effective filing date of any patent application subsequently filed. However, like patent applications, these documents will be kept in confidence by the Patent Office. If patent protection is desired, a patent application should be filed as soon as possible.

This program does not diminish the value of conventional witnessed and notarized records as evidence of conception of an invention, but it should provide a more credible form of evidence than that provided by the popular practice of mailing a disclosure to oneself or another person by registered mail. The program is made available as a service to those persons desiring to use it.

Content of Disclosure Document

Although there are no restrictions as to content, and claims are not necessary, the benefits afforded by a Disclosure Document will depend directly upon the adequacy of the disclosure. Therefore, it is urged that the document contain a clear and complete explanation of the manner and process of making and using the invention in sufficient detail to enable a person having ordinary knowledge in the field to make and use the invention. When the nature of the invention permits, a drawing or sketch should be included. The use or utility of the invention should be described, especially in chemical inventions.

The Disclosure Documents must be limited to written matter or drawings on paper or other thin, flexible material, such as linen or plastic drafting material, having dimensions or being folded to dimensions not to exceed 8½" by 13". Photographs are also acceptable. Each page should be numbered. Text and drawings should be sufficiently dark to permit reproduction with commonly used office copying machines.

A $10 fee is charged for filing a Disclosure Document. Payment must accompany the Disclosure when it is submitted to the Patent Office.

In addition to the $10 fee, the Disclosure Document must be accompanied by a stamped, self-addressed envelope and a separate sheet in duplicate, signed by the inventor, stating that he is the inventor and requesting that the material be received for processing under the Disclosure Document Program. The papers will be stamped by the Patent Office with an identifying number and date of receipt, and the duplicate request will be returned in the self-addressed envelope together with a warning notice indicating that the Disclosure Document may be relied upon only as evidence and that a patent application should be diligently filed if patent protection is desired. The inventor's request may take the following form:

"The undersigned, being the inventor of the disclosed invention, requests that the enclosed papers be accepted under the Disclosure Document Program and that they be preserved for a period of two years."

Retention

The Disclosure Document will be preserved in the Patent Office for two years after its receipt and will then be destroyed unless it is referred to in a separate letter in a related patent application filed within the two-year period. The Disclosure Document must be referred to in the separate letter by title, number and date of receipt. Acknowledgment of receipt of such letters will be made in the next offical communication from the Patent Office. Unless it is desired to have the Patent Office retain the Disclosure Document beyond the two-year period, it is not required that it be referred to in a patent application.

Instructions

PAGE 1 - Contains the general information needed to establish dates,

PAGE 2 - Permits inclusion of drawings or photographs which are needed to convey the design or function of the invention. If more pages are required, attach them to page 2. Some ideas are of such nature that drawings are unnecessary. In that event, leave Page 2 blank. Drawings and descriptions should be reasonably clear, providing enough detail so that a knowledgeable person can duplicate your invention. *THIS IS A DISCLOSURE DOCUMENT, NOT A CONCEPTION DOCUMENT.* It is no time to be secretive; let it all hang out!

SUGGESTION: Using carbon paper, you can easily trace a simple drawing onto Page 2. Then reinforce the carbon image with a black ballpoint or felt tip pen and clear up the reproduction with art gum or a soft eraser.

Drawings will vary in detail and complexity due to the differences and complexity of inventions. Firm guidelines are impossible. Just remember that the reader does not know about your invention - you are explaining it to him.

Patent drawings have their own format and formality, some of which you may as well use:

1. Where more than one Figure is needed label each clearly with numbers or letters - 1,2,3, etc., or a,b,c, etc.
2. Following the description sequence, assign reference numbers or letters to the parts as needed.
3. When the same part is used in two or more figures, always identify it with the same number.
4. Drawings should be dark enough to reproduce on duplicating machines. Xerox copies of pencil sketches are acceptable.

PAGE 3 - The description is a logical step-by-step explanation of the device. (See Patent #2,524,486, page 7.) (Rube Goldberg made himself and his drawings famous just by making his invention explanation clear, simple and amusing, but, of course, this is no place for fun or comic foibles.)

Completing the Process

1. Prepare one copy of the Disclosure Document and two copies of the Request Form.
2. Attach a $10 Money Order or check payable to the Commissioner of Patents.
3. Address your envelope to Commissioner of Patents, Washington D.C. 20231.
4. Enclose the two Request Forms, check or Money Order for $10 together with a self-addressed return envelope.
5. Mail the material by Certified Mail, return receipt requested.
6. One copy of the Request will be returned with a document number stamped on the first page. Have two (or more) photostats made and file away for safekeeping. Keep a copy of the Disclosure Document itself.

Warning as to Limitations

The two-year grace retention period should not be considered to be a period during which the inventor can wait to file his patent application without possible loss of benefits. It should be recognized that in establishing priority of invention an affidavit or testimony referring to a Disclosure Document must usually also establish diligence in completing the invention or in filing the patent application after the filing of the Disclosure Document.

Inventors are also reminded that public use or sale in the United States or publication of the invention anywhere in the world, more than one year prior to the filing of a patent application on that invention will prohibit the granting of a patent on that invention.

Let us add another cautionary note here. Among front-money invention promoters there is a move afloat to produce for the inventor a Disclosure Document for about $65. This is just another excuse for thievery. Most inventors do not need $65 worth of Disclosure Document. Most people, as a matter of true fact, do not even need $10 worth of Disclosure Document. The effective and less expensive way to handle the disclosure process is to complete Step 3 in lieu of Steps 1 and 2.

The Disclosure Document program is recommended only for those who have not kept a Journal or documented their date of conception.

STEP 3—The Inventors Journal

Note that the Journal is so important that it gets a multiplier asterisk on the Teach Board. This means that an invention, properly documented in a journal, is worth more than one that is not.

The purpose of the Inventors Journal is:

1. To establish your date of conception in the event you - or the purchaser of the rights to your patent application - are subject to "interference" proceedings (see Glossary).

2. To record the progressive steps in the development of your invention with relevant dates. Since in litigation the court will not accept an inventor's unsupported word, it will be necessary to rely on the quality of your records and the competency of your witnesses. A good record contains descriptions simply and clearly stated, so that even years later their meaning cannot be misinterpreted. It will also contain evidence of your thinking and, just as importantly, a record of your failures.

3. To show the diligence of your continuing effort and development. Lack of such diligence could cost you a decision. (See Ref. footnote Step 1.)

Dr. William B. Shockley of Bell Laboratories spoke of the importance of the Laboratory Notebook or the Diary Journal in establishing intellectual property ownership. When the patent is granted, this record will help the patent stand the test of time.

Dr. Shockley speaks specifically of the invention of the transistor. "A vital input to the preparation of this contribution (speaking of the transistor) came as a by-product of procedures at Bell Laboratories designed to optimize the advantages offered by the 'exclusive rights' in the Powers of Congress. In determining which of two competing inventors should be granted the patent, priority of conception and diligence are weighed heavily. The date of conception of the invention is usually established by the record of when it was clearly disclosed to and understood by a co-worker. Usually such endorsements by witnesses are made on pages of laboratory notebooks. These records are of vital importance in establishing facts in patent litigation. Consequently, information on the issuance and status of such notebooks is carefully maintained in organizations like Bell Laboratories."

(It should be noted that Dr. Shockley and his co-workers Bardeen and Brattain received one dollar each for their inventions, though a Bell official had said publicly that the transistor was worth a billion dollars. However, the three later shared a Nobel prize.)

The first five pages dated 23 January 1948 from Dr. Shockley's notebook, which contain the record of the conception of the junction transistor, are reproduced on the following pages.

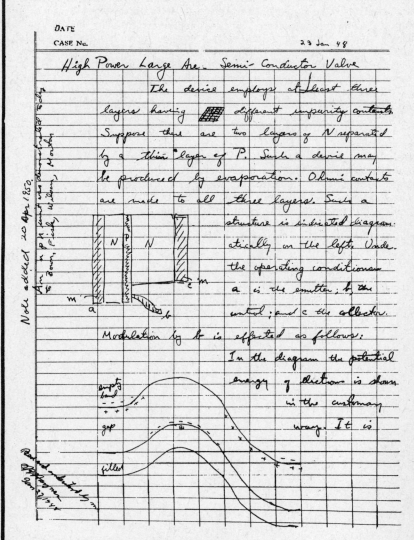

FIGURE 32. *The first of five pages dated 23 January 1948 from Shockley's notebook containing the record of the conception of the junction transistor.*

It proposes using evaporation for fabrication — a poor idea. But it does lead into the concept of minority carrier injection through a thin base layer.

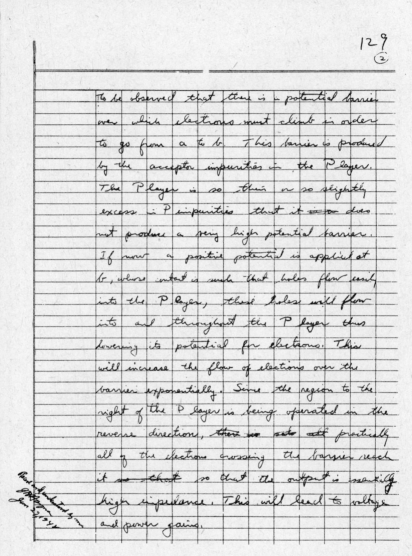

129
②

To be observed that there is a potential barrier over which electrons must climb in order to go from a to b. This barrier is produced by the acceptor impurities in the P layer. The P layer is so thin or so slightly excess in P impurities that it ~~is so~~ does not produce a very high potential barrier. If now a positive potential is applied at b, whose contact is such that holes flow easily into the P layer, these holes will flow into and throughout the P layer thus lowering its potential for electrons. This will increase the flow of electrons over the barrier exponentially. Since the region to the right of the P layer is being operated in the reverse direction, ~~there is set all~~ practically all of the electrons crossing the barrier reach it ~~so that~~ so that the output is readily high impedance. This will lead to voltage and power gains.

FIGURE 33. *The second page of the 23 January 1948 disclosure of the junction transistor.*

The basic amplifying considerations are clearly explained.

130 DATE

CASE No.   (3)

Some current will be drawn by control
electrode. However, this will be small compared
to the modulated current so long as the
concentration of holes in the P-layer is
small compared to the concentration of
electrons in the high concentration region
to the left of the P-layer.

This device can be made into a
structure of arbitrary extent in various ways.
For example, we can evaporate a layer of
N; then a half layer of P; then a grid
of metal; the other half layer of P; and
the second layer of N and the final metal
electrode. In this way a structure such as
that shown to the
left can be
produced.

It should
be noted that a particularly novel feature
is involved in this device. The current
path for the carriers of charge lies

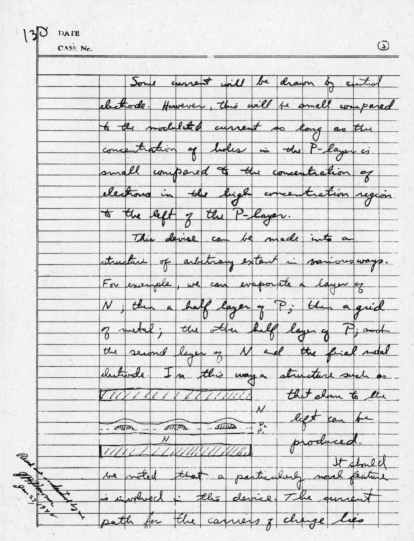

FIGURE 34.   *The third page of the 23 January 1948 disclosure including an appreciation of the importance of heavy doping of the emitter to reduce unwanted base-to-emitter currents.*

A half-baked idea about metal electrodes in the semiconductor to reduce base series resistance is discussed.

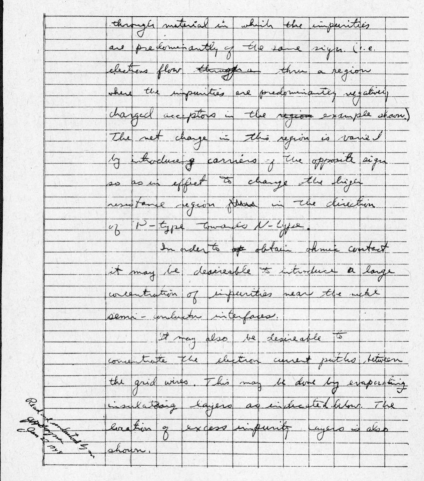

FIGURE 35. *The fourth page of the 23 January 1948 disclosure containing one idea that became a division of patent 5 of table I: the importance of heavy doping under the metal contacts to reduce contact resistance.*

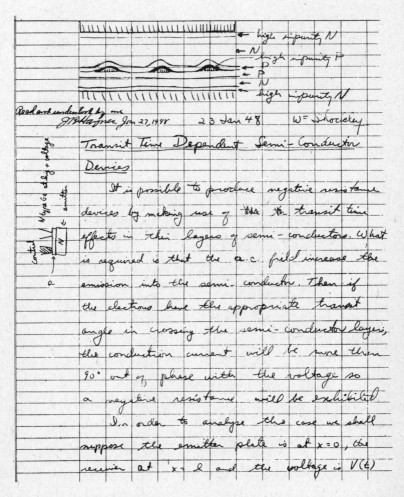

FIGURE 36. *The fifth page of the 23 January 1948 disclosure discussing what might be called "ribs" of high doping in the base. This diagram does not appear to follow what was called for on the fourth page.*

Also on this page is the start of a discussion dated 24 January 1948 of negative-resistance transit-time devices. This topic became a continuation in part of patent 5.

If you are not now keeping a Journal, you should obtain a stitch bound, page-numbered book. The pages may be blank or lined, according to your preference and convenience. Such books are available in college bookstores and some of the larger book and stationery stores. The Workshop also publishes one for the convenience of members.

Most businesses doing research require their engineers and technicians to maintain a Journal in which to record the development, experiments and test results of ideas related to the work they are doing. These records are periodically read and witnessed by management. All actions are dated. The courts tend to hold that if it is possible for a man to improve his advantage by cheating, he probably has, does and will, and the Journal does not lend itself to tampering.

Frequently inventors will have made some progress with their ideas before becoming aware of their need to maintain a Journal. If you are a new inventor, or if you have relied on the patent route and have not heretofore kept a Journal, you must start it with a summary of the history of activities to date, including information such as: (1) the date you conceived the idea, (2) the names of those to whom you have revealed the idea, (3) actions and experiments taken, and (4) any other evidence you have to support your past activity, i.e., receipts for purchases made for materials, parts or experimentation, etc. Receipts for purchases may be glued to the page, as they are usually dated and will lend support to your records.

Journal Rules

In completing your Journal, remember the following points:

1. Use black ink or a black ballpoint pen.
2. DO NOT ERASE! Line through and initial deletions.
3. If the page is bordered, all entries must be made within the border.
4. Write from edge to edge on each line, using a wavy line to finish incomplete lines and to finish blank lines.
5. Date and sign each new entry. Only one written entry is permitted per page. Do not record two or more inventions on a single page.
6. Keep all activities chronological - glue into the Journal drawings, sketches, receipts, photographs and other papers witnessed by someone you trust - someone who understands the invention.
7. Important elements of this procedure are:
   a. Description of concept, sketches and calculations.
   b. Progress (continuous and regular entries.)
   c. Reduction-to-practice, including results of experiments. INCLUDE FAILURES!
   d. Dates and completelly filled-in lines to prevent later alteration of entries.
   e. Witnesses.

Caution:

Contrary to some opinions, the Journal does not permit you to go on for years perfecting an idea with any guarantee that you can challenge someone else who has gone ahead and developed and marketed something based on the same idea. (Ref. Footnote Step 1.) The real test is diligence. The whole purpose of the patent system is to encourage the creation of new and useful inventions that will contribute to the betterment of our nation and life within it. However, a patent right is a negative one, since it is impossible to force an inventor to market his product. It guarantees only his right to prohibit others from making, using or selling his product.

STEP 4—The Preliminary Patent Search

Even though a patent may not be the right choice of every inventor, an incredible number of them have been issued by the Patent Office to date — over four million! If an abstract of each patent were put on an IBM card, there would be about three and a half stacks as high as the Washington Monument (555'). We are adding over 60,000 a year! That's a lot of ideas to search through. So although a patent might not be necessary for you, a patent search is.

The chance that your item is totally new is quite remote. After all, there have been only twenty-eight basic mechanisms invented sicne the beginning of the Industrial Revolution. However, if it is new, you can benefit by knowing that it is new. If it isn't new, you can still gain from this knowledge. But if your idea is too similar to a product already on the market you must admit its limitation and recognize the fact that trying to produce and market it would be a fruitless endeavor.

The cost of a preliminary patent search is an excellent investment. A professional searcher can quite rapidly identify and extract copies of the related art, and he may find infringing claims in patents that the inventor might never think to search out.

If money considerations force you to do your own search, there are patent libraries available in the larger cities. A listing is maintained in the booklet, "General Information Concerning Patents," which is published by the Patent Office.

Rick Comins, former Director of the Newhall Chapter of Inventors Workshop International, prepared some helpful guidelines on doing one's own patent search. "It is very time-consuming to make a patent search, but if you can find the time, it can be an interesting and illuminating experience, and the serious inventor should make at least one search during his career, so he becomes familiar with the system and its complexities", says Mr. Comins.

He continues: "For the novice who is trying his hand at a search, the librarian in the Patent Section of your library can be of great help. The Patent Room in the Los Angeles Library contains all patents issued since July 4, 1971. Patents prior to this date must be ordered from Washington. All patents issued prior to 1966 are on microfilm; since 1966 they have been recorded in books.

"When the inventor starts his search, he should record the time he enters the library and the time he leaves. Also note the number of patents dealing with your subject. This information could prove to be important evidence later.

"The patent search will only be as good as the individual makes it. The more concentrated his search, the better it will be.

"The first step is to list the categories to pursue. For example, take 'bell.' A bell is listed as:

alarm	indicator
warning	musical instrument
signal	annoyance(?)

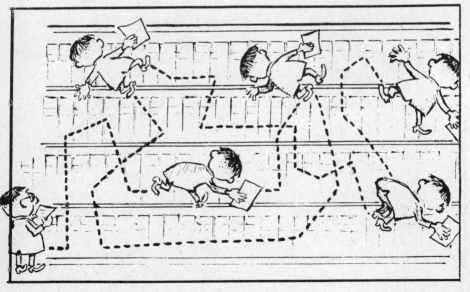

"Since 'bell' fits all of these categories, the search will involve all of these subjects. Once the categories are listed, the time consuming work begins. The first step is to refer to the Index of Classification, the official Patent Office book to Classes and Sub-Classes of categories of all existing patents.

Category titles range from —

Title	Class	Sub-Class
ABACUS	35	33
to		
ZWIEBACK	99	86

and fill nearly 400 pages. Some items may have more than one Sub-Class, as with CRANK CASE BREATHER which is listed in Class 92, Sub-Class 78. This means Sub-Class 78 is further broken down in the Manual of Class, to which the searcher must now refer.

"The manual contains numbers and titles of more than 400 classes and 66,000 Sub-Classes. It is divided into three main groups.

I. Chemical and RELATED Arts.
II. Communications, Designs, Radiant Energy, Weapons, Electrical and Related Arts.
III. Body Treatment & Care; Heating & Cooling; Mechanical Handling & Treatment; Mechanical Manufacturing & Power; Static & Related Arts.

"Classes distributed through these three groups range from:

Class	Title
1	No Class
through	
431	Combustion

You have to know what to **gopher**.

"Now, back to the bell. The Index Classification listing (under bell) would be:

Title	Class	Sub-Class
Bell	116	148

"Next, in the Manual of Classifications, under Class 116 (Signals & Indicators) there is the following:

Subject	Sub-Class
Bells	148
Sound Modification	149
Swinging	150
Pneumatic Actuation	151
Gong-Type	152
Doorknob contained	153
Rotary	154
Pivoted Striker	155
Multiple	156
Multiple Stroke	157
Rotary Striker	158
Lever Operated	159
Plunger Operated	160
Escapement	161
etc....	etc.

"So, if you define your big idea as a plunger-operated, rotary striker, multiple stroke, pivoted striker, gong-type bell, you would find it under Sub-Class 160 of Class 116. This is an example of what the Manual of Classification can do.

"The searcher now refers to the Annual Index — Patents publications. Herein are all patents issued by years according to Classes and Sub-Classes. An example: we will look up "Pivoted Striker, Gong-Type Bell," Class 116, Sub-Class 155 of above Manual of Classification. In 1969, Index of Patents, we see no sub-class 155 listed under 116, Signals & Indicators. So, there were no patents issued under this subject in 1969. But in 1970 there was one patent issued — No. 3,529,567.

This procedure must be done for each year to cover all patents of a Class and Sub-Class. Once a patent number is found, the last step is to look it up in either the book or microfilm entitled, "Patents Specifications & Drawings." The foregoing patent number turns out to be a Mechanical Fire Detection Alarm Device, complete with 16 drawings, eight claims and abstract. Also, four pages of how it works and what it's for.

If the results of your search show that the patents most similar to yours do not contain the same description or claim the same features as your invention, you can proceed with more confidence, and you will have justified the time and expense. If you find that your idea was patented years ago and is now in the public domain, this merely means that the idea is available for marketing, if you still favor that course.

If we recognize that many perfectly good ideas have been born before their time, we can understand why they didn't reach the marketplace. Technology and materials have been constantly improving, and advertising and distribution systems now make it easier to get a product on the market. Such new methods and improvements may make an old item practical today.

Although creative people have a potential worth that should not be wasted in recreating an old idea, it is nonetheless possible to produce something from the past by improving it, or putting it on the market at a better social or economic time, and the item may succeed now where it failed before.

Contacting the original inventor and asking him a lot of questions may result in your obtaining valuable information. Find out why he thinks his idea didn't succeed. Are his tooling or other production items still in existence? Amazing bargains are many times available; tooling, patent sale, inventory or a struggling business which you may turn into a success.

Interpretation of the language found in the claims uncovered in patents may require the professional help of a patent agent or attorney. The language is often technical and challenges understanding to those unfamiliar with it.

Don't fall for $5 or $10 searches. These are just a come-on by the quick-buck promoter.

In closing this section, we cannot overemphasize the importance of a prelminary search. The results are always meaningful. They show an idea is:

    a. worthy of continued work and expense, or

    b. in the public domain (to repeat, the product may be a profitable one today, even though it did not suceed before, and money that you would have put into protection can be put into production instead), or

    c. contained in another patent still in force. Learning this, you save additional development expenses on an item subject to infringement...in which case you had better consider other business alternatives.

STEP 5—Models

Making Intellectual Property Tangible

Tangible means touchable and, in the case of inventions, there is a special term - "Reduction to Practice" - which is used to imply tangible. At one time all patented inventions required models, but that requirement was dropped in favor of an adequately described invention. "Adequate" means that someone familiar with the art could duplicate the invention just by using the description. And, of course, that is just what the patent is - a document designed to convey this knowledge to the public.

It may or may not be necessary to make a working model, but before doing so, simple logic involved in the situation will decide if a model is to be made before or after a patent search. The Teach Board, Position 10, calls for model making decision.

A patent search will cost you a day or so at a patent search facility if you do the search yourself, or $150-$400 fee to a searcher for doing it for you. A good search will uncover patents on inventions similar to yours, and it will also disclose if your specific invention has already been patented. Think ahead. A search early in the development of your idea may save you the expense of a costly working model, or it may influence the way you design your machine. However, if there is ANY question as to whether your invention will work, or whether you have adequately refined the design, a working model should precede the search. The reason for this is that the model that evolves may be so different from your original that the original searcher might not have covered the exact art area. Similarly, a patent should never be applied for prematurely. There are far too many patents pursued before the invention is adequately developed and the expensive patent, when issued, is worthless. Step 5 will discuss the patent search process.

The Teach Board suggests that a working model be made as a general rule, but as with all things, generalities are not always true. Many large scale inventions wil require the Teach Board steps to be conducted in theory the first time(s) through to determine proper action,

The subject of models, prototypes and flyers and their interrelationships is expanded here.

The purpose, importance and use of models, prototypes and flyers are not well understood by most novice inventors. In years gone by it was required that a model be produced to obtain a patent. This was defined as "reduction to practice." Today "reduction to practice" is usually acceptable in written form, in your Journal or a Patent Application. It is assumed that it is possible to describe a device and its functioning, or a process or a method, with sufficient accuracy so as to establish the feasibility and workability to someone accomplished in the art. For example, a chemical formula could be made clear to a chemist without the need for the use of actual chemicals. An electronic circuit could be explained to an electronics expert without using any electronic components. This has occasionally lead to invalid claims, but on the whole, it greatly simplifies the patent procedure.

Models

Models still serve a significant and useful function. Frequently a model does not perform quite as well as expected in theory and the preparation of a model results in a series of improvements in form, function and, possibly, simplification. And it is tangible. The potential buyer is usually more willing to put up money for something that he can see and feel and operate. This is particularly true of complex mechanical devices. At some point of increasing complexity, it again becomes difficult or impractical to produce a model and the project is again better treated theoretically. You can be sure a great many people understood the atomic bomb before it was reduced to practice.

However, when a model is desirable, don't try to make the first model in its ultimate material, particularly if the material is inflexible and difficult to work with.

After you have done your paperwork thoroughly, try making your first model out of cardboard. It costs about half a second and no money to move the location of a hole, but if you have to drill a hole in your ultimate material, or paint something or cut something off, you have not only wasted your time, but you might also have interfered with other phases of your model.

Dr. John E. Gorrell, member of Inventors Workshop International, not only suggests cardboard, stapler and thumbtacks for the initial model, he also suggests using different colors for the mechanical parts and different color for the wiring. "It can save hundreds of dollars spent in fussing around and coming up with wrong answers and wasting a great deal of time. Cardboard moving models are infinitely better than a whole ream of drawings which show Mode A, Mode B, Mode C, etc. There is a great deal you can learn by working things out with your own hands. If you are not mechanically inclined, then get somebody who is. But don't have a baby and expect somebody else to raise it...it won't end up the way you want it."

After you have worked the bugs out of your idea by the use of an inexpensive cardboard model, you can build your final model with more assurance and less waste and loss of motion. A functioning model will better demonstrate the workability of a principle and permits experimental variations and also establishes dimensions, shapes, function and materials. It inevitably results in refinements and improvements that will make a patent, when issued, much stronger.

Prototype

Most inventors are well advised to make a prototype and then try to improve it — redesigning it if necessary — and even to consider very seriously the prospect of going into the business of its manufacture. The reasoning is simple. The invention that is in production and sales takes on far greater importance than one that is not.

Prototypes are models which are made to verify some phase of design or production before a design is "frozen" for production. In complex systems, only a small number of prototypes are made up at a time, so that remaining bugs can be located and corrected in a subsequent run. A prototype usually requires tooling and is a finished working model of your idea.

Flyers

A flyer is a single-sheet information release. In some cases it is cheaper and more suitable to use flyers in lieu of models, but flyers are usually required even if you have models. A properly designed flyer will frequently eliminate the need for sales promotion models. There are very few items which cannot be adequately explained and "sold" with a good flyer.

Brochures

Brochures are a form of flyer, usually in the form of a pamphlet, and customarily printed on higher quality glossy paper, used by a person or company to market a product.

STEP 6—Decision Time

You have completed the preliminary steps of protection, and now you are faced with an important decision — what direction to take from this point. It's time to back away from your invention or idea and take a really objective look at its potential. This is a time when an evaluation by someone knowledgeable may really pay off. Inventors Workshop does a guidance analysis for its members which is most helpful in bringing an objective view to your future actions.

The Teach Board concentrates on the "Guidance Analysis" in Blocks 22-36. This is the heart of decision-making and should be carefully followed and thoroughly researched. Objective opinions are necessary, and determining relative merits may require interim testing, development of models or parts, detailed drawings or other special activity which cannot be shown on the Teach Board. But anyone clever enough to invent something new certainly should be clever enough to know what is necessary to PROVE feasibility of function.

Block 22 addresses model function. "Model" may be theoretic (math) as well as physical. By using your particular project in this evolution you'll know if you can proceed or not. Either give up and start a new project or redesign. Similarly, Blocks 23 and 24 represent other degrees of success rather than failure. As a game to teach the interrelationships of these elements, a dice throw selects the next move, but in real life, you perform tests to determine where you are and what your next move should be.

"Feasibility of Fabrication" enters frequently into new products. Many products are "30 years too soon" because the technology or materials aren't yet available. It is vital to determine, as early as possible in the life cycle of an idea, whether it will be producible with today's technology at a price consumers will be willing to pay. Great ideas and excellent products must sometimes be abandoned, because it is not economically sound as a product. Consumer items are particularly sensitive. Furthermore, if you develop and manufacture a product that has a marginal profit but good acceptance, you are very apt to watch competitive designs evade your art (and patent) and beat you at your own game! It is vital to understand that when done ethically, this is the essence of the free enterprise system. You must not only get ahead, you must stay ahead.

Blocks 29-32 address the patent search issue (also discussed above as related to working models). These blocks almost duplicate blocks 12-16. It is important that the issue be raised in each case, and evaluated in the light in which it appears. In both cases, a seldom discussed circumstance is found when a search reveals similar prior art. Consider the possibility of licensing from the original patent holder. All too often the patent holder has not been able to launch his dream machine successfully. He may have inventory and tooling, or he even may have died, and his widow doesn't know what to do with the "thing." In any event, the patent search is always informative, educational and frequently surprising, and you will gain new respect for our nation's inventive genius!

Blocks 33-36 introduce the concept of market researching, and the results of the market research are as important to decision making as having an invention which works. There is a saying that "nothing happens until something is sold," and that is so true that we cannot, as inventors, proceed on the assumption that our invention is so obviously valuable, we will automatically become millionaires. WE MUST KEEP OUR FEET ON THE GROUND WITH OBJECTIVE ANALYSIS OF THE REAL WORLD SITUATION. This is the most violated principle in the inventor's world. The sooner this lesson is learned, the sooner an inventor will find success. Another truth, when understood in all of its concomitant aspects is that "profit" is the necessary ingredient to any product success. So dwell on the big picture by looking at it from every angle and aspect, and to begin, conduct a market research program.

If you can study and really understand and are willing to put forth the energy required to do a mini market research, you will be successful as an inventor, because you will cast off the failures, and you will modify and evolve the promising inventions to make them successful.

First, let me pre-sell you on the concept of market researching. If you can consider for a moment that you CAN be wrong, or that you COULD BE MORE correct, and you are willing to find that out, we can begin.

But bear in mind that even expensive and intensive marketing programs can fail. The Edsel car is a classic example. (If you can find a copy of Vance Packard's "Hidden Persuaders" you are in for an entertaining evening's reading.)

The most exotic market research programs can, and frequently do, fail to get the BASIC DATA. Stripped of all of its mystique, the elements of basic data are quite simple and direct.

There is a simple approach introduced by IWI and used by hundreds of inventors to enable them to find out for themselves the truth about their product. It is a standard procedure and, when understood and followed, will give standard results. It is good, it is effective and it is a MOST IMPORTANT TOOL for you to utilize as an inventor.

The procedure requires that you have something to show to the prospective consumer or manufacturer. This may be a rendering of what you have invented. It may be a scale model, or it may be a prototype. But since conducting successive market researches as the invention moves from mind to market is recommended, whatever you have at this stage should be used. The feedback will help move you to the next step! Clearly, the better it looks or the better it functions, the better results you can expect, so don't be sloppy. Do as professional a job as you can.

Blocks 37-40 of the Teach Board identify, in broad terms, elements of the invention game rarely considered by the inventor. This is unfortunate because they are not only a part of the invention business but they are a part of a complete package. You've seen the cartoon of the child sitting on the pot captioned, "The job isn't complete till the paperwork is finished!" This was designed to emphasize that paperwork is required for every product — and invention is no exception. It is a hard lesson to learn if you haven't been associated with manufacturing. Somewhere in the early (preproduction) life cycle of EVERY PRODUCT, production drawings were made, specifications were spelled out and production planning and engineering were accomplished. The simplest plastic product that can be envisioned required these steps.

You, the inventor can increase your rewards by doing all you can for yourself and by hiring experts to do what you cannot. Hiring experts is an investment in your future. Learning to qualify them is critical. IWI, through its chapters and its computer program tries to maintain a list of people and businesses who have been recommended by satisfied customers — i.e., other IWI members. But wherever you find your help — check for references if there is any question.

When you have accumulated a great deal of objective information about your product or process, you now need to consider "How shall I market this?"

Please notice the emphasis on NOW. "NOW is well into the Teach Board. We haven't yet addressed the Teach Board Route 17-21 because, ideally, the route just described should be travelled first. Without the benefit of Steps 22 through 40, the real value of the invention will not become visible, and the merits of a patent application not known. A patent is a very expensive piece of paper just to display. You are now ready to consider the final factors in the decision.

At this stage you must decide if you want to go into business, authorize someone else to use your invention or abandon it altogether. Abandonment is the only route that will not cost money or effort. In making your decision, try for honest objectivity. Probably 50% of the ideas that get to this point should be abandoned with no additional expenditure of time and effort.

A few facts and factors are offered to help you understand the problem:

1. *Perhaps immediate application for patent is premature at this point.* It is too expensive to take this route without first determining that there is a market for your product. On the other hand it may be the **ONLY** suitable coverage for some inventions.

2. *What about sale or licensing, with the buyer assuming the responsibility for ongoing protection?* This is the path inventors would lazily prefer but there is danger involved. We reiterate that Patent law allows only twelve months in which you may disclose, sell, offer or use your invention publicly **BEFORE** applying for a patent on it. If you don't apply within this period, your invention falls into public domain. A year may seem a long time in which to find a buyer to assume the patenting responsibility, but contrary  to the propaganda offered by unethical promoters, selling your invention is neither easy nor fast. Not many companies are able to make quick decisions. Also, some of those who are looking may have very little conscience when Corporate Profit is involved.

Your item must not only be good, but you must be prepared to negotiate from a position of strength based on firsthand knowledge. You must **KNOW** about tooling costs, production, delivery costs and profit potential. You must become an expert about your invention.

Start a business

Of the 50% of the inventions that survive the test and are to be offered for sale, something like 90% of the remainder will derive a better measure of success if put into actual production by the inventors themselves. Rights to an invention that has been manufactured and sold are far more valuable than similar rights to one that has just reached the prototype stage. A very large percentage of new ideas and inventions are simple enough to tool up and produce, so the inventor can either set up his own production system or sub-contract the work.

However, with a finished product, the inventor then faces the problems of marketing. Section II of this Guide book is devoted to that phase of operations.

Preliminary Marketing Analysis

Based on the foregoing work to become objective, there are other elements to crank in now.

A limited production run will often reveal more reliable information than a more expensive marketing analysis.

Before proceeding, ask yourself again these important questions: Can the item be priced to allow sufficient markup to make it profitable for the people handling it?

Will distribution costs be out of proportion on a continuing basis? Can

41

you afford to leave products with a retailer on a consignment basis? What about the cost of display materials? Most of all, are you sure your item will be satifying a need at a reasonable price?

Correct pricing is very important. Too high a price tag might make the prospective buyer feel the item is not worth the money. Too low a price tag, and he might dismiss it as junk. You must find the "Natural Selling Price (NSP) for your item and then convince buyers that it satisfies their needs.

An example comes to mind of Frank O. Armbruster of Campbell, California, who developed a puzzle which he called Instant Insanity. He made some samples and played with them until he was convinced the puzzle was fun, and then he showed it to his friends. They, too, enjoyed it. Convinced he had a worthwhile idea, he proceeded to develop a technique for manufacturing at a reasonable cost. To find its "Natural Selling Price" (NSP), he offered it for sale at different prices — 69 cents, $1.00, and $1.25. — and found that he sold more at $1.00 than at any other price, a price at which the buyer felt he was getting value for his money. The price was right, and he built up sufficient sales to interest Parker Bros., the game manufacturer, to whom he sold his rights.

If the NSP can be five or more times the cost, you have a potential winner. It is interesting to note that a higher price is frequently better than a lower one, because it conveys the feeling of value to the buyer.

A product with an NSP of *five or more times* manufacturing costs will fit into a heavy middleman structure — rack jobbers, distributors, wholesalers, direct salesmen, etc.

A product with an NSP of *three* times manufacturing costs will sell through a mail order agent or mail order house.

A product with an NSP of *two times* manufacturing costs will only sell through the efforts of the manufacturer who retains all the profits.

Example #1

If you, as an inventor, license to a manufacturer and distributor and you get a 4% royalty — can you afford to go for a patent and develop the product?

Item: Toothbrush

Potential market 210,000,000. (Estimated number of users in U.S.)
Resale — once a year.

Manufacturing costs, labor and materials, etc.	$ .08
Manufacturer's selling price (Three times cost)	.24
Royalty	.0096
Wholesale Price (plus 25%)	.30
Retail Price (plus 40%) (NSP)	.42

Assume annual sales based on 1%, 5% and 10% of market capture.

	1%	5%	10%
Sales	2,100,000	10,500,000	21,000,000
Royalty (.0096)	20,160	100,800	201,600

Questions:

1. Can the manufacturer produce the item for 8 cents?
2. Will the product capture 1% of the total potential market?
3. Is one-year replacement resale reasonable?
4. If less than 1% of the market is reached, can I afford to risk patent costs?

If your answers are yes—your item has good prospects.

Example #2

If you as inventor, license a yard winder to a manufacturer and distributor, and you get 5% royalty, can you afford to develop a good prototype and pay patent costs, etc?

Item: Yarn winder—estimated life 20 years—no resale

Potential market	10,000,000
Probable sales	10,000
Manufacturing costs	$8.00
Royalty 5%	.40

Assume total sales as a percentage of total market capture

	1%	5%	10%
Sales	1,000	5,000	10,000
Inventor's cost to			
develop & print	$2,000	$2,000	$ 2,000
Royalty	320	1,600	3,200
(−)	$1,680 (−)	$ 400 (+)	$ 1,200

Questions:

1. Is the market potential realistic?
2. Is the manufacturer's cost estimate realistic?
3. Is there any possibility of cash and royalty?
   (The answers here are critical. Be sure you arrive at the right conclusions before you proceed with patent costs.)
4. Is there a possibility of starting a business of manufacturing and selling directly?

Assume that the retail price is:	14.95	
Units of sales are	5,000	10,000
Gross Sales amount to:	$74,750	$149,500
Tooling and Production	$80,000	$ 80,000
Advertising and Misc.	20,000	20,000
(loss)	$25,250 (gain)	49,500

It would appear that a royalty sale is not practicable, but direct sales may yield a net profit worth some effort if the projection of 10,000 sales is realistic, but questionable or impractical if the sales figure projected is a lesser amount.

Example #3

Item: Safe Handle for Bank Vaults

Potential sales, new banks only	100 per year
Manufacturing cost	$100
Royalty	$ 10

Even if you could capture 100% of the market, you would only realize $1,000 per year. No matter how great the idea, it is probably not worth patent search or patent application, but it may be marketable as an idea disclosure, under contract.

Summary

By now you should be able to appraise your chances and decide which direction to take. If not, restudy this step or get some help to explore the marketing picture further.

STEP 7—Patent Application (now or later)

Let us say that your progress so far has measured the market and proved to you that your idea is worth examining more thoroughly and that proceeding to patent is worthwhile or necessary to protect your rights.

We will assume that with a new and novel item, as determined by the search, you have reasonable assurance that a patent can be obtained. It is time to take a hard look at this Step. You must decide if (1) you want to (or can) sell your license at this stage and let the buyer do the patent work in your name, or (2) you want to go into production and business yourself. According to the definition in the patent statute, an invention can be patented if it is a "process, machine, manufacture or composition of matter," or any improvement thereof. For purposes of clarity, let's define the terms.

A PROCESS is a method of producing some new physical result or an old physical result in a new and better way.

A MACHINE can be defined as a device or combination of devices utilizing energy or performing an operation.

MANUFACTURE covers just about anything made by man. It must be a physical element — and not a product of nature.

COMPOSITION OF MATTER is the result of intermixing two or more ingredients to get a product that has properties different from those of the ingredients individually. The product could be a mechanical mixture or a chemical compound.

ANY IMPROVEMENTS THEREOF means a step forward in the particular art or science.

The statute also requires that the invention be new and useful — that it have some utility and that it be novel.

The statute states further that a patent may not be obtained if the invention is obvious to a person having ordinary skill in the discipline or art to which it relates. That is, the invention must show a degree of ingenuity not expected as normal for a skilled craftsman.

An invention cannot be patented if it was known or used by others prior to being conceived by the inventor in question, i.e., the invention was described in a printed publication prior to conception date or one year before filing an application; or the invention was in public use for more than one year prior to filing application. An invention is considered to be in public use if it is performing its intended function and its use is not controlled by the Inventor. An invention is considered in the experimental stage if delays in filing application are caused by a bona fide effort on the inventor's part to bring his invention to perfection and to make sure that it performs the job that it was intended to do.

An invention described clearly enough to be copied in a publication anywhere in the world one year before filing an application cannot be patented. However, the publication must be printed and available to the public. Manufacturer's internal publications, not available elsewhere, are not considered public publications.

a. Protection under Steps 1, 2 and 3 afford the opportunity to approach possible buyers, manufacturers or other businessmen with minimum risk.

b. You can make the item and sell it for one year in order to test it out before you invest in the patent. This is the best route for perhaps 75% of the inventions produced by individual inventors and will be dealt with in Section II — Pursuit of Success.

c. You can go for a patent solely because you feel it is the only safe way to approach many of the larger companies with inflexible disclosure agreements, or because you believe the scope of your invention is too broad to risk exposure without patent.

Before making patent application, however, consider the following extract from a Small Business Administration Bulletin:

"POINT OF CAUTION

While the advantages of obtaining a patent are fairly obvious, it must be recognized that a number of pitfalls and obstacles lurk in the path of every application. For example, a patent by no means guarantees immunity to lawsuit, but rather sometimes seems to attract challenges as to its legality. As one patent lawyer has said, 'A patent is merely a fighting interest in a lawsuit.'

1. Most foreign countries will not grant a patent if an idea has been publicly disclosed before application is made in their country. But there is little choice since without exposure the chances of selling are very slim.

2. Exposure is always a risk even after patent.

"INTERFERENCE

One of the pitfalls in applying for a patent is interference (occuring in less than one percent of the cases) when two or more applications have allowable claims for substantially the same invention. Since a patent can be granted to only one applicant, the parties in such a case must give proof of the date the invention was made.  The applicant who proves that he was the first to conceive the invention and produce a working device will be held to be the true inventor. If no other evidence is submitted, the earliest date of filing the application is considered the significant criterion. Priority questions are determined on evidence submitted to a Board of Interference Examiners.

"INFRINGEMENT

Unauthorized manufacture, use or sale of patented property constitutes infringement. The patent owner may file suit in a Federal court for damages and/or an injunction prohibiting the continued use or manufacture of his patented article. If an item is not clearly marked 'patent...(number), the holder of the patent may sue for damages on account of infringement but no damages can be received covering the period before the infringer is so notified. Moreover, no recovery of damages is possible for any infringement occurring more than six years before the filing of the complaint. And there is no established method of learning of any infringement of a patent. A clipping service and a sharp eye for references in trade literature may be helpful, but the responsibility lies entirely with the inventor.

"FOREIGN PATENTS

If you wish to market your patented product in a foreign country, you should apply for patent protection in the particular country to prevent infringement. See 'General Information Concerning Patents' for further details, or consult a patent attorney or agent who can assist in obtaining patents in other nations for American clients.

"OTHER PROBLEMS AN INVENTOR CONFRONTS

Even though an invention passes the expert, impartial judgment of a patent examiner as to novelty and workability, it still must be commercially acceptable if the inventor is to make money from it. In this respect one should not expect help from the Patent Office, as it can offer no advice on this point.

It is interesting to note that in modern technology the vast majority of patents granted are merely improvements or refinements on a basic invention.

Changes in size, shape, adjustability, portability or materials are not patentable unless the changes produce startling or unexpected results. Individual parts of the invention must cooperate to perform some new function; some new result must be produced. Also, the mere replacement of an element of the invention with another known to be capable of performing substantially the same function as the element replaced will preclude allowing of a patent. (See Glossary — Patent.)

Therefore, since the claims allowed on an improvement patent are narrow, as compared with those of a basic patent, the inventor runs a proportionately greater risk of infringement if a basic patent is in force.

Here is an example: Inventor George Westinghouse patented an entirely new device — the air brake. For this he was given broad protection by the Patent Office. Suppose that later, inventor 'B' had devised a structural improvement, such as a new type of valve for the compressed air. Since 'B' would have received relatively narrow protection on the valve, he would not have been able to manufacture a complete air brake without infringing Westinghouse's patent. Nor could anyone else to whom 'B' licensed his patent make the whole brake.

While it is possible for the inventor to pursue his/her own patent application, the retention of a good patent attorney or agent is highly recommended, because patent procedures can be complicated. The technique of writing strong claims is a highly developed art. The strength of the patent can be measured by the Claims.

In some cases, the Small Business Administration can offer sound advice.

"THE PATENT APPLICATION

In the United States the patent application must be filed in the name of the inventor. If there is more than one inventor, a joint application is made. Even the application for a patent on the invention of a company's employee must be filed in the inventor's name.

Often employment agreements require an employee to assign to the employer any invention relating to the employer's business. Even without such an agreement the employer has a 'Shop right' to use free of charge an invention developed on the job by an employee.

The patent application must contain the following five parts:
1. Specification or disclosure of the invention;
2. Drawings, if the invention "admits to" drawings;
3. Applicant's oath or declaration;
4. Applicant's signature, nationality and address;
5. Appropriate fee.

The exacting requirements of the Patent Office for a patent application are described in the Rules of Practice of the United States Patent Office, which may be purchased from the Superintendent of Documents, Washington, D.C. Currently these are published in a 200-page book titled "Code of Federal Regulations 37" (37CFR). The construction of the invention, its operation and its advantages should be accurately described.

From the "specification" of the application any person skilled in the field of the invention should be able to understand the intended construction and use of the invention. Commercial advantages — which would be attractive to a prospective manufacturer — need not be discussed.

The claims at the end of the specification point out the patentable new features of the invention. Drawings must be submitted according to fairly rigid Patent Office standards.

Who Can Apply for Patents

Only the inventor (or his legal representative) can apply for a patent; the only signature on an application is his. An attorney or agent is appointed by, and acts for, the inventor.

While applying for a patent is a specialty business, and it is not highly recommended for the individual inventor, reports have come to us from the Patent Office that they tend to be extremely helpful and less critical of patent applications made by the individual inventors themselves. Each individual must evaluate his own ability and confidence to make such an application.

PROTECTION SUMMARY CHART

To Protect	Form or Method	Comments
Conception	Date of Conception Form	This form is, as soon as possible after inspiration, witnessed and notarized.
Conception	Disclosure Document Program	Filed with the Patent Office (not a Patent Application) - costs $10.
Invention Construction or Composition	Patent Application	Good for 17 years granting. May be filed by attorney, agent or inventor.
Invention Appearance	Design Patent	New and ornamental - original. Three-and-a-half, 7 and 14 years and then reverts to public domain.
Invention Appearance	Copyright	Works of art, etc., cheaper than a design patent, not for things of "utility".
Trademark Service Mark Certification Mark Collective	Patent Office Registration and with individual states	Must not be easily confused with another mark or product, nor can it be simply a surname or just a description. This is good forever. Examples abound - Ford, DuPont, Chevrolet, Studebaker, etc.
Package	Patent	A functional construction
Package Design	Design Patent, Registration as Trademark	The Coca-Cola bottle is a protected shape.
Leaflets	Copyright	

To Protect	Form or Method	Comments
Labels	Copyright- Trademark	Must be accurately descriptive and usually carries trademark, logo, etc.
Title of Periodical	Trademark	
Title of Book	No special method	Might have protection against unfair competition.
Direct Mail	Copyright	
Radio and TV Programs	Copyright	Also see last item below.
Slogan	Not Protectable	
Merchandising, Selling Plan Advertising Ideas, etc.	No special way to protect	Good original ideas can be sold under a contract agreement. See "Protection of Unpatentable Ideas." Section I-Step.
Written Descriptions, Promotionals and Other Supporting Materials for above.	All methods, depending on materials	Frequently, adequate development of the supporting sales aids, materials and other supporting materials make up the "saleable package".
Dramatic and Musical Compositions, lectures and oral addresses	Copyright	May be coypright protected. Special consideration permits a manuscript for oral delivery to be deposited with the Register of Copyrights. Other manuscripts are protected under common law until published.
Game	Trademark, Patent, Copyright	Rules of games not patentable. Apparatus may be. Can copyright instruction booklet, and register name as trademark ("Monopoly").

STEP 8—Handling and Intangible Idea

It is a common saying in the business of idea development, invention promotion and patent circles that an idea alone is worth nothing. This is generally true. However, as with all generalities, there are exceptions. Everything starts with an idea. Nothing can emerge or develop or come into being without it.

Many ideas are potential blockbusters in profitability to business or industry. If the idea is valuable, it should be protected when marketed.

A classic story comes to mind about an idea sold to the Diamond Match Company. It's never been substantiated, but it does illustrate the point. An entrepreneur approached Diamond Match Company with a proposition that if they would pay him a lump sum of $50,000, he would show them how to save $100,000 a year. It was a very interesting proposition, and the company decided to accept his offer. An agreement was entered into, and the entrepreneur unveiled his suggestion that the company put sandpaper on only one side of their large match boxes instead of two sides, as they had been doing. The man was paid his money, and to this day Diamond Match is saving $100,000 (or more) a year simply by having removed the sandpaper from one side of the match box.

Ideas are visible in everyday sales and promotions; advertising is always looking for new ones. For example: "Ford has a better idea." "Progress is our most important product." "Ask the man who owns one." "Ask the person who drinks it black." "His Master's Voice." "Time to retire." These are ideas that paid off. Maybe just in salary, maybe in a lump bonus payment. It's immaterial. The point is that ideas, business plans, methods or systems — if they can make money — are worth money. But it takes ingenuity to get them across and working.

And it is a difficult path. Most large manufacturers have built-in fences to protect themselves from law suits. 1) They want the inventor to sign their nonconfidential disclosure agreements which, while variously worded, generally leave all considerations of reward or payment to their discretion. The inventor must depend on the strength of his patent, copyright or trademark for protection. 2) Companies have staffs of people who are charged with the responsibility of introducing their own new products. 3) Industry and commerce generally work on projects several years in advance. Five-year planning is common. 4) There are many in high echelons autorized to say "No," but only a few who can say "Yes."

In selling an idea, care must be taken to adequately document every stage. Record all details with sketches, diagrams, calculations, drawings, charts and other materials needed to demonstrate that the idea has potential value. This implies, as is intended, that a great deal of work goes into preparing for disclosure of every intangible idea. Date, sign and have witnesses date and sign documentations. Keep the Inventors Journal up to date at all times. Offer your idea by letter with a request for approval of a confidential disclosure. The letter might read something like this:

Gentlemen:
I have a new and novel idea which could effectively and economically promote your new product to the senior citizen.

My studies and evaluation of the merit of the idea are based on the statistic that 48% of this group are in or near the poverty range. With my idea, you can conservatively capture 3% of this group. The cost for reaching them with your message would be approximately $300,000 under my plan, and the net return on the investment is projected to be 27%.

If you find these figures interesting, please sign and return both copies of the enclosed agreement form, and I will promptly forward complete details of my idea.

Sincerely yours,

Your Name

The letter is the final step in the chain. Because it is backed by development records and other documentation, you are selling a supported idea.

Study the Protection Summary Chart on pages 55 and 56 and find the method that fits your needs.

SECTION II
IN PURSUIT OF SUCCESS

It is not the purpose of this Guidebook to be a guide for going into business, but it is a guide to help inventors realize the fruits of their labors. Facets of the inventor's dilemma are examined in this Section, so that the Inventor who takes the time and expends the effort (or the money to have the work done by others) will truly be rewarded.

While this Guidebook is intended for all who are able to read, experience has taught this writer that frequently an inventor is unable to view his invention objectively. As a result he become more vulnerable to a con artist's get-rich-quick scheme, because he and his invention are so emotionally linked. He frequently will waste several years of his income proving how right he and his invention are.

If you recognize these traits in yourself, be doubly careful in your pursuit of success.

You need not become a sheep among wolves — or one of the wolves either, for that matter. Just remain true to yourself, using your God-given intellect, and play a fair and winning game.

Part 1
MAKING, USING AND SELLING

A patent is property. It grants the right to prevent others from making, using or selling things covered by the claims in the patent. Income tax laws are designed for the free enterprise society in which we live. There are distinct tax advantages to being in business. If you are not in some sort of business venture for the tax advantages it affords, you are not taking advantage of the system. Just remember that you are an inventor, and you are in the business of inventing.

The following check list will help you to decide and evolve the best course of action for yourself. Use any source of information you can find. Go to the library, talk to your accountant or tax advisor, then roll up your sleeves and get to work.

The following questions, properly answered, will give you the necessary insight to get your business going. Admittedly, they require your making an educated judgment and sometimes require consultations with experts in one field or another. Answer each question with complete candor and honesty. The inventor who doesn't is committing a wrong against himself.

Market Analysis

1. Who specifically, will buy the product?
2. What is the size of the market?
3. What percentage of the market can you hope to capture?
4. Is the market base expanding?
5. Will your item be profitable in these markets?

The Product

1. Is your product ready for production? (Production engineered?)
2. Will it remain competitive if product line is expanded or product improved?
3. Have objective evaluations been made of the design and function?
4. Who will produce the line?

Distribution

1. Have you any experience in distribution?
2. Have you any firm commitments from distributors to handle the item?
3. How much time do you have to devote to distribution?

Operations

1. Are marketing goals, production and cash flows laid out?
2. Are all sources of supply identified and committed?
3. Are cost control and accounting responsive to need?
4. Chart all data.

Cash Flow

1. What is schedule and amount of money input? Source committed?
2. Is return on investment equitable to all investors? Is it adequate?
3. Are your projections adequate?

Ownership
1. Who owns how much of the operations? Who controls?
2. Is ownership compatible with investment, responsibility and creativeness?

Sales

1. What volume of sales do you expect?
2. What percentage is this of the total market?
3. Where is your break-even point, and when will it be reached?
4. Chart all data for visibility.

People

1. What are the realistic qualifications of management and supervisory personnel?
2. Do they have adequate direct or related experience?
3. Are the duties and responsibilities of the hierarchy (Organization tree) adequately defined?
4. Are the members of the Board of Directors strong in related fields?

Part 2

PRIVATE OWNERSHIP, PARTNERSHIP AND CORPORATION

If you are in business, you will come under one or the other of these classifications. There is a lot of material available in the public library that describes in detail the various forms of business, their relative merits and drawbacks. As an inventor you have a special viewpoint to consider, and we will explore your options briefly.

Private Ownership

If you have not entered into any agreements with others, your business is private and solely your responsibility. You will buy, sell or trade and report to the government. You can be sued and relieved of all of your earthly possessions if you are found to be at fault.

Partnerships

When two or more have entered into a partnership agreement, it is a private ownership except that all partners are liable and share all liabilities. Conversely, a partnership is extended credit because the assets of all partners are possible collateral. There are arrangements, however, in which "limited" partners are vulnerable only to the extent of their liability and voice in operations.

Corporations

A corporate setup immunizes the corporate owners and stockholders from any personal financial liability. It has many advantages and some disadvantages. It is more tightly controlled by the government and is generally more highly taxed. It is used by most large operators.

Part 3

GOING INTO BUSINESS

As an inventor, you have, as mentioned before, some special problems which should be recognized when you give consideration to whether or not you should go into business. You are considering a high-risk operation, with less than 10% chance of recovering your expenses. You must invest a great chunk of time, energy and money in proving out your failures as well as your successes. This is acknowledged by the tax people and is the key to the business and tax decisions and the form of business you enter.

Very few inventors can go it alone. They frequently require some help and financial assistance, and sometimes it is necessary to take on partners to get a worthwhile invention going. Forecasting the costs is difficult and considerably less precise than starting an uncomplicated laundromat. Experimental failures, with success elusively around the corner, can change an inventor's viewpoint in midstride. He should try to look ahead and prepare for any emergency before it arises.

Inventors invent to satisfy an inner need to create, with the hope that they will one day catch the brass ring. And there are brass rings to be caught - and now and then a solid gold one, too. Investment money is always on the lookout for the inventor who has a good thing. Your form of business will influence the availability and terms for venture capital.

Inventors are sometimes greedy. Far too often a reasonable man becomes unreasonable as soon as he sees the color of gold. And sadly, but understandably, this often kills a reasonable deal. Don't let an overinflated opinion of the value of your idea spoil a sale for you.

A corporation representative came by the IWI office one day and told us of an inventor and his brother who had developed a modification for a carburetor which would make it more effective. The corporation was seriously interested in the product and entered into negotiations. But as soon as the inventors realized they had something that someone else thought was good enough to buy, they suddenly began to make impossible and impractical demands. They wanted a corporation formed in which they were to hold prominent offices, such as President, Vice President or Chairman of the Board. Like Aesop's fable of the dog with a bone who saw his own reflection in the stream, and thinking he saw another dog with a bone, snapped greedily at the reflection, only to drop the bone he had, and lose all.

An inventor's "Necessity Level" will vary from time to time. One's independence of action is affected by the form of business and housekeeping involvement with that business. An inventor can too easily become a noninventing executive, and he can be left at the post while a more clever executive takes the race. Know your talents and limitations, and get others to do what you can't do well.

A similar story is told by another IWI member who is a successful inventor of toys. When approached by a fellow member, he agreed to present the man's toys to one of his company contacts on the east coast. The company was interested in the product, but they took their time making a decision. The inventor, without confiding in anyone, had his attorney contact the company to find out why it was taking them so long to come to a decision. The company was so upset, it returned all papers and disavowed all interest and threatened the member that if he ever sent anybody else like that to them again, they would do no further business with him.

Companies don't need headaches, and inventors must understand the necessity of accepting a reasonable offer on a first invention. He will gain stature by exercising patience and reason. And remember, it is the very nature of the inventor to invent. There is an unlimited store of new ideas, and you shouldn't be too concerned about any given one of them.

Has the above served to stimulate you to examine yourself without bias? Are you psychologically able to relate to the many requirements of the business world? A well-written book which we recommend highly is "Think and Grow Rich" by Napoleon Hill. Do not be misled by the titled reference to wealth. Read it. The principles that Mr. Hill has distilled into this book cover just about the total philosophy of man. A bibliography of helpful books and source data can be found on page 101.

Part 4

TAX ADVANTAGES OF BEING IN BUSINESS— AND OTHER TAX CONSIDERATIONS

As pointed out in **PART 3**, there are, indeed, many tax advantages in business. Tax laws are in your favor, so you are missing an opportunity if you do not examine the system and, if possible, become part of it. For example, the law allows a deduction of a percentage of your rent or house payment if you have your business in your home. Telephone, water, electricity, maintenance, car mileage, postage expenses can be divided between your personal and business activities. The only requirement is that you keep substantiating records. You must be prepared to defend the cost ratios you claim. Since this is a free society that encourages its members to be productive in a capitalistic way, the special interests of businessmen have helped to create laws supporting their special interests. Until these laws are changed — if you can't beat 'em, join 'em.

As an independent inventor, you will sometimes have to decide whether to go for short or long-term gains. If you do not know which would benefit you more, consult your tax advisor. Since Internal Revenue rules are not totally clear on many points, it may be wise to seek the Department's advice. For one thing, you will learn if it is to your fiscal advantage to deduct your expenses each year or if you should accumulate expenses until the invention is marketed. The latter is the sounder choice  for the highly successful item, and the former if your invention has turned out to be less than a blockbuster. Best dreams notwithstanding, about ninety percent of inventor-marketed items will end up as losses a should be charged off on an annual basis. Don't let your optimism overide your good judgment. Consult your tax advisor and the IRS.

Part 5

CONTRACTS AND AGREEMENTS

Understanding contracts, agreements and their applications frequently involves great difficulties for the novice businessman. The cost of getting advice from an attorney is frequently quite high, but the consequences of a poorly-written agreement can be even higher. Good judgment must be exercised in determining when to hire legal counsel and when it is an unnecessary expense. The determination is not easy. But if you have a good relationship with your attorney, he will be more apt to give you advice when

needed. If you go to your lawyer only infrequently, he will probably charge you the top fees. But it's like preventive maintenance — it is better to pay a few bucks for advice before you need it than to be sorry after.

The subject of contracts is more fully explained in Section V — Contracts.

Part 6

OFFERING YOUR ITEM FOR SALE

When an item has been developed to the point of saleability, there are techniques of offering it for sale that afford the inventor a better chance of success than a bumbling, unknowing approach. When you first expose your article, it should be presented in such a way that it excites the viewer's interest without really disclosing what you have. Your prospective buyer can determine his own interest, without having a disclosure forced on him before he's had the opportunity to consider what you have to sell.

The appearance of your presentation should be given a lot of your attention. You don't want to turn him off before he has a chance to learn the merits of your invention.

John Todd, inventor of the "Dyna Diver," marketed by Parker Brothers as the "Sea Diver," used an excellent technique in his presentation. He wrote the following letter to several companies.

December 10, 19--

ABC Manufacturing Company
Address
City, State

Attn: New Idea Department

Gentlemen:
On the advice of a local toy retailer, I wish to introduce to your firm an invention which has received extremely favorable response in a number of confidential exposures.

Description

Briefly, the invention (patent presently pending) could be described as a self-contained, hydrodynamic assembly, approximately 5x5x10 inches in size, capable of numerous functions within a closed, subaqueous environment. Although primarily of the table or desk-top variety, it can be used with equal facility anywhere, indoors or outdoors. It is adaptable as an educational aid as well as to any one of the many and varied toy designs which hold appeal for consumers of all ages. A few suggested applications include:

1. Simulated underwater digging or mining operation.
2. Simulated depth bombing.
3. Simulated underwater construction.
4. Demonstration of basic hydrodynamic phenomena.

ECONOMIC FEATURES

To the consumer this represents a highly desirable yet relatively inexpensive toy which involves no recurring operation costs (such as batteries, steam, chemicals, etc.).
To the manufacturer it offers a low-risk investment. As stated by one seasoned toy retailer and retired manufacturer:

"...the projected retail price to manufacturing cost ratio of 10 or 12 is extremely attractive, and its appeal is further enhanced by the increased publicity in oceanography."

This type of toy is new to the industry, since its producibility became economically feasible because of a recent advancement in one special technique. All parts can now be manufactured expediently, using automatic equipment. The only remaining details are those necessary to tailor the toy to specific application.

PUBLICITY

Numerous periodicals have published accounts of the increased activity in underwater research, e.g. "U.S. NEWS AND WORLD REPORT," March 30, 1970, comments on the multibillion-dollar annual business in oceanographic research, development, food and mining production. This expanse of publicity and expenditure of financial resources can only perpetuate active interest in toys associated with submarine activity, just as the recent moon shots bolstered sales in space-oriented toys.

Should your firm be interested in a working demonstration, I would be happy to arrange an appointment for such demonstration, and to answer any questions that might occur to you.

Respectfully yours....

John Todd

You will note that the manufacturer was given a fairly good idea of what he had without disclosing his invention. John Todd has given us probably one of the finest examples of how to handle an invention — from conception to market. He thoroughly engineered, developed and prototyped his product. He had complete drawings, samples and specifications of his item to turn overn to the buyer so that they could produce it with minimal preparation or expenditure of engineering funds. Study this letter carefully; you will find his technique invaluable.

SUMMARY: You haven't all the data yet, but most of the factors which should influence your decision making at this point have been introduced, and the remainder of the Teach Board should fall into place. We will continue to examine additional facets of the mind to market activity important to the inventor.

SECTION III

TRADEMARKS

Trademarks are in many respects most valuable as a "protection" device. A registered trademark gathers strength with use and is not limited by time. They can be seen around us in abundance — Coca Cola; Ford; Chevrolet; Borden's Elsie the Cow; etc. etc.

A trademark identifies the goods of a particular company, distinguishing them from the products of other manufacturers. Trademarks become closely associated with particular products. It is this association that makes them valuable and protectable.

When a product is first introduced, it is a good idea to have it identified with a catchy name and a symbol which can become associated with it.

It is also smart — right at the outset — to sell your product interstate. Invoice it and record payment in order to qualify for trademark application. Don't go overboard by investing heavily, however, in printing decals, etc. until a trademark search has been made.

There is a classic story told that concerns the use of the *KIWI* shoe polish. Shortly afte WWII an oriental company began to manufacture a shoe polish of very poor quality, and they took the *KIWI* as their trademark. This trademark, however, had been used for years by an established company in Australia who made a very high quality shoe polish. The Australian manufacturer brought suit, enjoining them from further use of the *KIWI* on the basis that the use of their trademark on an inferior product was damaging to their business. They won the suit. Whether or not they were also awarded damages is unknown, but the story illustrates the value of an international trademark.

There are other marks, such as "Union Made," which are Certification Marks. This may appear in other forms such as: "Made in Texas — by Texans," "Assembled by the....," or "A Product of the Dominican Monks."

Yet another type of mark or slogan is that associated with services performed, such as "KXTC-XTC, where music makes the difference." "Progress is our most important product," "The Spirit of '76 Lives at Union Oil," "Let your fingers do the walking." These slogans are called "service marks."

A Collective mark is a mark representing a group. It is often associated with a trademark phrase, such as "A member of FDIC" or "FTD Florist."

Examples of trademarks are easily found in the telephone book, particularly in the yellow pages. You can readily pick out those which you have learned to associate with certain products or service sources.

It is not the purpose of this Manual to offer expertise on the subject of trademarks but to stimulate you to get your invention or idea to the point where it may become important enough to need a trademark.

Unlike patents, rights to trademarks are acquired by use. Registration of a trademark alone does not create exclusive rights.

A quick and inexpensive way to get a preliminary check on the novelty of a trademark is to consult the "Trademark Register" in a large library. This is a commercially published $40 book about the size of a telephone directory which lists all the registered trademarks by name in alphabetical order. Following each name is its registration number. Pick out the pertinent numbers and order copies of the trademarks from the Commissioner of Patents and Trademarks, Washington, D.C. 20231. The Register will show the mark, the owner and the class of goods for which it is registered.

An inventor decided on the name "Innes" for certain tools he sold to the electronic industry. The Trademark Register showed only two other "Innes" marks, one for shoes and one for farm machinery. He is not likely to have any problems unless his enterprise becomes big; but then he can afford to pay lawyers. The old Packard Motor Car Company once sued the Packard Electric Company (transformers) for trademark infringement; the court held that there was no infringement because the goods sold were so different that they would not confuse the public. On the other hand, Kay Electric Company once sued Kay-Lab, both manufacturers of electronic instruments. Kay-Lab lost and had to change its name; it chose "Kin-Tel."

A Trademark Register check may be all you need when you're starting out. If the operation gets big, you will need a trademark lawyer, because on the higher business levels the matter becomes complicated.

SECTION IV

COPYRIGHTS

Copyright literally means that the owner is the only one who has the "right to copy" or authorize copy of his own work.

If you write about the corner gas station and copyright the printing of your story, others cannot "copy" it without your permission. That is not to say, however, that they cannot cannot also write about the same gas station in their own way. This principle applies to writing, works of art, books, periodicals, speeches, music compositions, maps, photographs, prints, illustrations, motion pictures, music recordings, statues, etc.

All unplished work is protected under common laws from the moment of its creation, but this protection ends when the work is published. It must then be given the protection of a statutory copyright by publishing it with a copyright notice.

74

The Copyright is a "Bundle of Rights" implicit in the Constitution, Article I, Section 8 "...securing for limited times to authors and inventors the exclusive right to their respective writings and discoveries." The Copyright Law was greatly revised and approved by Congress in 1976 to become effective 1 January 1978. The new law includes exceptions to the exclusivity provision with new provisions for some compulsory licensing.

Further, it changed the duration of the U.S. Copyright to the inventor's life plus 50 years, in lieu of 28 years and renewable for 28 years.

New forms for registration are provided also and are detailed below.

"Fixation" replaces "publication." "Fixed" is a replacement for "published" because of the need to include recordings, both visual and audio presentations over TV and radio. "Published" has also been awkward to use when referring to sculpture art.

It is not the purpose of this Chapter to make readers experts on the national and international complexities of Copyrights but to point up the purpose and use of the law to the business of inventing and creating. Much misinformation has been circulated. An otherwise ethical inventors group was advocating the copyrighting of a Disclosure Document as a means of protecting an invention and somehow this advice still crops up from time to time. Just remember that a Copyright is a right to control the making of copies of writings, works of art and music. It is thus significantly different from a patent.

An excellent reference work by Harry G. Henn, "Copyright Primer," was published by the Practicing Law Institute and is recommended for anyone wanting or needing to examine the entire subject.

It is recommended that anyone trying to determine whether or not he can be helped by copyright simply assume that he can, and that he affix a copyright notice on all of his writings or creations. It is inexpensive, serves notice and may prove useful later. It is suggested that it be a practice to so mark everything that is printed.

If you properly mark a bumper sticker which says "I Am A Domestic Engineer" and illustrates a housewife with a broom, you can restrict anyone from copying your art. You must understand, however, anyone can restyle the printing and do a different illustration and not violate your rights.

Let's briefly examine copyrightable "Works of Authorship" which must contain at least some intellectual effort and originality. It cannot be copied from works of others. There are seven categories:

1. Literary Works
Works, other than audio visual works, expressed in words, numbers or other verbal or numerical symbols or indicia, regardless of the nature of the material objects such as books, periodicals, manuscripts, phonorecords, films, tapes, discs, or cards, in which they are embodied."

2. Musical Works, including any accompanying words

3. Dramatic Works, including any accompanying music

4. Pantomines and Choreographic Works

5. Pictorial, Graphic and Sculptural Works

Includes "Two dimensional and three dimensional Works of fine, graphic and applied art, photographs, prints and art reproductions, maps, globes, charts, technical drawings, diagrams and models — insofar as their form but not their mechanical or utilitarian aspects are concerned."

6. Motion Pictures or Other Audio Visual Works

Motion pictures are defined as "Audio visual works consisting of a series of related images which, when shown in succession, impart an impression of motion, together with accompanying sounds, if any."

Audio Visual Works are "Works that consist of a series of related images which are intrinsically intended to be shown by the use of machines or devices such as projectors, viewers, electronic equipment, together with accompanying sounds, if any, regardless of the nature of the material objects, such as films, or tapes, in which the works are embodied."

7. Sound Recordings

"Works that result from the fixation of a series of musical, spoken, or other sounds, but not including the sounds accompanying a motion picture or other audio visual work, regardless of the nature of the material objects, such as discs, tapes, or other phonorecords, in which they are embodied."

There is another class of materials which is **EXCLUDED** from copyright (but may qualify for protection under patent or trademark):

1. "Any idea, procedure, process, system, method of operation, concept, principle or discovery, regardless of the form in which it is described, explained, illustrated or embodied in such work."

2. "Works of the United States Government." This includes published or unpublished work of employees of the government as part of his official duties. Anyone is free to use any of the works of the government. Important distinction is made in the postal service publications that include stamps, and in the case of some of the Congressional parliamentarians.

3. Trademarks, ideas, plans, methods, systems, inventions, computing and measuring devices, names, titles, short phrases and expressions, general ideas or outlines for radio and television programs, blank forms, slogans and phrases.

There is still another group of materials which are indeterminate and when the Copyright Law was revised, these were left for future determination. Typeface styles and ornamental designs were deferred, as were the writings of the National Technical Information Service publications. This group comprises unfinished business which the Congress elected to bypass in order to pass the new law.

ELIGIBILITY

Almost anyone who will be using this Handbook will be eligible for protection under Copyright, because the coverage is so broad.

"Unpublished" works tend to be covered by a blanket "without regard to the nationality or domicile of the author and without regard to place or publication."

"Published" works bring in boundaries somewhat to identify "national origin" because of eligibility of author or the eligibility of the work.

"Published" works gain protection if:

1) Author(s) is a national or domiciliary of any nation which is a party to a copyright treaty to which the United States is a party, or is a stateless person.

2) Work was first published in a country that was then a party to the Universal Copyright Convention.

3) Work was just published by the United Nations or agencies or the Organization of American States.

4) Works within the scope of a Presidential Proclamation.

OWNERSHIP AND MADE-FOR-HIRE

Frequently when two or more collaborate, or when someone writes for hire, or as an employee, or is commissioned to do a work of art to collaborate in the production of a work, his position isn't as clear as if he were the sole party to the materials. He has reason to become concerned with the rights of ownership. The answer is not simple and clear.

In the case of "Joint Work" the respective rights are not covered by Copyright Law but left to other "decisional" law.

Works made for hire are considered to be authored by the employer unless otherwise defined by a written agreement. There is a special definition of works "specially ordered or commissioned." If they are to be included as works made for hire, however, they must be one of the following:

1) A contribution to a collective work.
2) Part of a motion picture or an audiovisual work.
3) A translation.
4. Supplementary work (introduction/conclusions etc., for example).
5) A compilation.
6) An instructional text.
7) A test.
8) Answer material to a test.
9) An atlas.

Anything not covered by these nine categories needs to have a written agreement if it is to be considered — for hire.

Works for hire differ from individual material in the way they are treated in the statutes:

1) Eligibility of the work for Copyright is based on the eligibility of the employer, not the writer.

2) Duration is for 75 years from publication or 100 years from creation, whichever expires first.

3) Not subject to termination conditions.

4) Renewable provisions, if applicable, are by the employer/proprietor etc. and not by the heirs and assigns.

5) Works for hire are not exempted from importation restrictions (with some exceptions).

Needless to say, there are a great many complications, unresolved or cloudy elements left for future clarification and resolution. Some of these may be important to individuals, but for the most part it is for more complex situations; if you find you have anything other than clearcut, simple copyright, be sure to consult a specialist in Copyright Law. A paragraph from the Copyright Primer does much to identify your rights.

"When an 'individual author's' 'ownership of copyright,' or of any of the exclusive rights under a copyright, has not previously been transferred voluntarily by that individual author, no action by any governmental body or other official or organization purporting to seize, expropriate, transfer, or exercise rights of ownership with respect to the copyrights or any of the exclusive rights under a copyright shall be given effect. This provision is to counteract seizure of American copyrights of foreign authors, especially dissidents, or by foreign governments to suppress the works."

It is necessary that your copyright be recorded in the Library of Congress before you institute suit for infringement. It is no longer critical to have a Copyright notice on your work, if omitted in error (with certain limits). It can be corrected within five years; however, it is not wise to take chances which can be so simply avoided. Put the Copyright notice on everything you publish. It is simply:

1) "©," "Copyright" or "Copr."
2) Year of first publication.
3) Name of the "owner of the copyright" in the work.
4) "All Rights Reserved" may be added to cover contingencies that may arise from the Buenos Aires Convention.

The location of the notice is not specified but is usually in front of most publications.

REGISTRATION

Registration of a Copyright is the action of submitting to the Copyright Office:

1) The appropriate form (discussed below)
2) $10, and
3) Two copies

There are five basic administrative classes, each with its own application form. These are:

1) Class TX — Nondramatic literary works. The category is very broad. Except for dramatic works and certain kinds of audiovisual works, Class TX includes all types of works written in words (or other verbal or numerical symbols). A few of the many examples of nondramatic literary works include fiction, nonfiction, poetry, periodicals, textbooks, reference works, directories, catalogs, advertising copy, and compilations of information.

2) Class PA — Works of the performing arts. This category includes works prepared for the purpose of being "performed" directly before an audience or indirectly "by means of any device or process." Examples of works of the performing arts are: (1) musical works, including any accompanying words: (2) dramatic works, including any accompanying music: (3) pantomines and choreographic works, and (4) motion pictures and other audiovisual works. This category does not include sound recordings.

3) Class VA — Works of the visual arts. This category consists of "pic-

torial, graphic, or sculptural works," including two-dimensional and three-dimensional works of fine, graphic, and applied art, photographs, prints and art reproductions, maps, globes, charts, technical drawings, diagrams and models.

4) Class SR — Sound recordings. With one exception, "sound recordings" are works that result from the fixation of a series of musical, spoken, or other sounds. The exception is for the audio portions of audiovisual works, such as a motion picture soundtrack or an audio cassette accompanying a filmstrip: these are considered an integral part of the audiovisual work as a whole.

5) Class RE — Renewal registration. For works originally copyrighted between January 1, 1950 and December 31, 1977, the statute now in effect provides for a first term of copyright protection lasting for 28 years with the possibility of renewal for a second term of 47 years. If a valid renewal registration is made for a work, its total copyright term is 75 years (a first term of 28 years, plus a renewal term of 47 years). Example: For a work copyrighted in 1960, the first term will expire in 1988, but if renewed at the proper time the copyright will last through the end of 2035.

SECTION V

CONTRACTS

Contracts

Contracts and agreements are such a common part of everyday existence that we are almost unaware of our involvement with them. There is a large body of law to protect the parties to agreements, both written and unwritten: At one time an oral proposal of marriage was regarded by the courts as a binding agreement. If you asked her, "Will you marry me?" and she answered, "I will," you could be sued for breach of promise

if you later decided you didn't want to. Although the agreement was unwritten, it was no less binding.

You call your grocer and have the delivery boy bring your order to the house. In accepting and paying for the groceries, you are entitled to expect the quality and quantity you ordered and paid for. If inspection reveals either damage or shortage or substandard quality, the grocer could be liable by law to make an adjustment or replacement.

COMPETENCY OF PERSONS

A contract with a person who was drugged, drunk, insane or mentally retarded at the time the contract was executed can be challenged and would probably be found invalid.

Illegal agreements cannot be enforced by law. For example, "contracts" such as are credited to the Mafia are considered illegal.

Verbal contracts are limited by certain dollar amounts.

Contracts require signatures and witnesses, with at least partial payment and acceptance of earnest money as binder.

An agreement or meeting of the minds is contained in the terms and conditions stipulated.

A period of time is necessarily stipulated.

Each agreement should be tailored to the situation. Preprinted agreements never really fit.

"Sale" is the transfer of ownership of property — whether it is a house, car or invention — subject to liens or claims by others, based on prior investment, sale or licensing. The purchaser of full rights to a protected invention can legally prohibit anyone, even the inventor, from making, using or selling the invention. When patented inventions are involved, the sale must be registered in the Patent Office within three months. It is reasonable for a buyer to put sale money into escrow for a period of three months in order to safeguard himself from the possibility that the invention has been sold and licensed to others.

Contracts are only as good, or as strong, as the agreement between the parties. If the parties are not interested in making an agreement work, or if they are actively interested in rupturing the agreement, the contract will fail.

A contract, then, is defined as an agreement, and its principal benefit is to identify the areas of understanding. Some of the conditions that could affect the validity of a written or unwritten agreement are set forth here.

SELLING AND LICENSING AGREEMENTS

Almost every novice in the invention field is ignorant about the way inventions are licensed or what payment is fair. There is probably a great deal of misinformation about invention contracts, because often neither buyer nor seller is highly motivated to tell how much or how little was paid or received. In some cases the amounts involved could be a source of embarassment, or conversely, the amount of money paid by a buyer might provide leverage to subsequent inventors in their negotiations.

The business of selling and buying is as varied as the items traded and the personalities involved in the trading. We will try to examine the subject in sufficient depth so that the average inventor can relate himself and his product to accepted and acceptable contract terms. Generalities are often dangerous and misleading and extremes are too unrealistic for most situations, so we must examine the middle ground.

For some time now there has been a growing tendency to slight the inventor's contribution — to reward him for his work either inadequately or not at all. To an ever-increasing extent individual initiative is being stifled by the growth of the corporate entity. Some of the unconscionable acts committed in the name of corporate profit are unbelievable — until they happen to you. In total, they may well prove to be the single, most easily identifiable betrayal in American history. If, as this writer believes, it was the Patent system and the reward for individual creativity that made America great, then the conditions under which an inventor relinquishes control of his creation are critical.

Inventors must become knowledgeable salesmen of their own products if they are to gain greater benefits for their efforts. With information as the key, we can hope that each new "good deal" will inspire his own expertise in the seller's market. If this book contributes to that end, it will have served its purpose.

84

So let's get into sales and licensing agreements. Here are some different types:
 —Individual
  —Partnership
   —Trust
    —Holding Company

There are advantages to each one, depending on circumstances. The Individual Agreement is most common and least expensive. It covers the conditions under which the invention is used in a single industry whereas the trust agreement permits an inventor to use one industry to help open his market to other industries.

The Partnership Agreement means the invention is assigned to a partnership, and if the inventor is a partner, he receives his income from the proceeds of the partnership. It can be ideal for family relationships in which one dominant partner runs the business and the income is split according to agreed percentages.

The Holding Company Agreement is similar to the Trust, but more complex, It provides certain tax advantages but can lead to losses unless one has knowledgeable help in the preparation of the contract. Several questions should be given careful consideration in the preparation of an agreement, and each answer should be based upon your needs.

1. Is the agreement between the inventor and a buyer or a licensee? Is either a corporation? If so, the state of incorporation must be shown.
2. Is it a sale agreement or a licensing agreement? Exclusive or nonexclusive? For what territory or industry or limits?
3. What is the amount of binder — the initial payment?
4. Is further protection to be obtained, i.e. patent, copyright, trademark (U.S. or Foreign)? Who will pursue and pay for such action?
5. What is being sold or licensed? An item? Process-related secrets? Future developments? Access to records? Inventor's support?
6. Is the inventor to be available as consultant?
7. What are the terms and conditions of payments? Cash? Installments? Minimum payment? Minimum performance? Royalty percentage year by year? What is the basis of computation? Is cumulation of excess royalty permitted?
8. What is the frequency of accounting and access to records for audit?

9. What are the conditions and rights for termination? What happens to ownership of invention patents and evolved ownership during the life of the invention prior to termination? What termination causes are considered acceptable?
10. Can buyer or seller assign interest to rights?
11. What are the obligations or rights to sue? Who assumes the expenses and responsiblity for recovery in the event of infringement?
12. Is the product indentification by patent number or trademark?
13. In case of a settlement dispute, which state laws apply? Will the ruling of the American Arbitration Association be accepted?
14. Are the addresses of principals included, as well as the responsibility of parties to keep addresses current — for notices and other exchanges?

Since it is our goal to "get a clear view of the obstacles," let us examine the chief obstacle to equitable contract terms. The inventor is usually his own worst enemy. He either lacks the experience, gets greedy, or finds some other way to spoil what could have been a fair deal. This happens too often to be ignored.

Let us explore an Agreement. The following sample has been designed to include the more important conditions and terms which may be found in Agreements to license or sell patents, inventions and other products of the mind.

LICENSING (OR SALES) AGREEMENT (1)

This agreement by and between John J. Jones, hereinafter called inventor, and Preston Products, Inc., a California Corporation (2), hereinafter called Licensee (3) is effective on the........day of ...., 19........ (4).

WHEREAS Inventor represents and warrants that he is sole (5) owner to all rights and interest in the Invention called .... (6) and elsewhere suitably defined and described (7), bearing patent application number .... (8), referred to hereafter as ....

WHEREAS Licensee represents and warrants that it is financially able to meet the terms set forth herein and is desirous of securing an exclusive license (9), and Inventor is willing to grant such License under the terms set forth herein.

WHEREFORE, in consideration of the sum of ....dollars ($........) hereinhand paid (10) by Licensee or Inventor, receipt of which is hereby acknowledged, Inventor and Licensee agree as follows:

I. Inventor hereby grants to Licensee sole and exclusive world rights (11) except the State of Alaska (12) to manufacture, use and sell the Invention called .... for the life of this Agreement.

II. This Agreement shall endure for the life of the patent, unless sooner terminated as hereinafter provided.

III. The Licensee shall pay Inventor during the term of this Agreement a royalty of five percent (5%) (14) of the net sales price (15) on each and every item sold. For the purpose of this Agreement, net sales price shall be defined as "gross sales price" less credit allowance for returns of unsold or damaged merchandise, discounts allowed for sales incentives, taxes and shipping costs, as shown and accounted for in customer invoicing and account records.

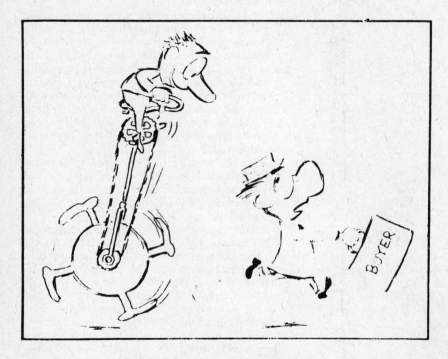

IV. Licensee shall make royalty payment accompanied by accounts every three (3) months (16) not later than the last day of January, April, July and October of each year for the duration of this Agreement.

V. Licensee shall keep true and accurate records of account available (17) to Inventor and his agent or representative for inspection at reasonable times at Licensee's principal place of business.

VI. Inventor grants a six (6) month period (18), if such period is needed, for tooling, production and distribution before imposing a minimum performance. Therefore, the first minimum quarterly payment of five thousand ($5,000.00) dollars (19) shall become due and payable no later than the last day of October, 19 . . . . (20, 21).

VII. Improvements to this Invention by Inventor (22, 23) shall be basis for renegotiation (24) of the royalty terms of this Agreement and thereafter shall inure to the benefit (25) of the Licensee. Improvements to this Invention by Licensee (26) shall inure to the benefit of the Inventor (27) under the terms and royalty contained herein.

VIII. Licensee shall diligently pursue patents (28) for any improvement or additional patentable features and to file for other protective measures (29) such as copyrights and trademarks (30), if and when appropriate.

IX. Licensee shall apply statutory patent and trademark (31) identification to all production under terms of this Agreement, the rights of Licensee to the use of the trademark having been separately negotiated (32) and documented.

X. In the event of infringement (33) Licensee shall prosecute (34) at his own expense and shall receive any settlement (35) therefrom; agreed royalties shall continue to accrue (36) to Inventor.

XI. In the event of infringing claims against (37) Licensee, Licensee shall defend (38) the Invention at his expense. If such claims result in the determination that this Invention is infringing on the rights (39) of others or that the patent is invalid, the Licensee shall have the option of cancelling the Agreement or of negotiating a nonexclusive Agreement (40).

XII. Licensee shall have the right to sublicense (41) to others the rights and obligations (42) contained herein, subject to the approval of the Inventor. (43).

XIII. Licensee agrees not to attack directly or covertly the validity of the Invention so at to force renegotation or cancellation of this Agreement. (READ FOOTNOTE #44 on this Section.)

XIV. This Agreement is not transferable (45) except with the approval of Inventor and shall be binding upon and inure to the benefit of the heirs (46) or successors to the parties.

90

XV. Failure to pay royalties (47) when due, or to maintain minimum performance (48) shall be cause for termination (49) of this Agreement by Inventor, at his option (50). It is also agreed that in the event that Licensee becomes bankrupt or insolvent (51) or should change ownership, it shall be lawful for the Inventor to revoke this license (52) by notice to Licensee (53) served by Registered Mail to the last address (54) acknowledged by Inventor. It is also agreed that any breach of agreement (55) by Licensee shall be corrected within 30 days (56) of notice by Inventor that such a breach has occurred.

XVI. The services of the Inventor as a consultant (57) shall be available to the Licensee on a part-time basis (58) and the compensation therefor shall be Fifty ($50.00) Dollars per hour (59) plus expenses.

XVII. If the services of Inventor are required on a full time basis (60) the compensation shall be Thirty Five Thousand ($35,000) Dollar per annum (61). Any inventive creation shall be subject to royalty negotiations (62).

XVIII. All monies herein are quoted in U.S. dollars (63) and shall be deposited in a Note collection account (64) to be established by the Licensee in the Fidelity Bank, Fifth and Main Street, Encino, California.

XIX. The interpretation (65) of all the conditions of this Agreement shall be to sustain and enforce (66) this Agreement. If any point of agreement is found unenforceable (67) all other points of Agreement will still be considered in effect.

XX. Any dispute or disagreement (68) not resolved by the parties to this Agreement shall be submitted to the American Arbitration Association (69) and their judgment shall be final. The cost (70) of such arbitration shall be shared equally (71) by the parties hereto.

XXI. This Agreement is subject to interpretation and enforcement under the Laws of the State of California (72).

XXII. Any notice (73) or other communications shall be sent to the addresses shown (74 below for Inventor and Licensee. It shall be the respective responsibility of each of the Parties to notify the other by Registered Mail, Return Receipt Requested, of any changes to these addresses during the life of this Agreement.

Footnotes:

(1) This type of agreement can be used either as a Licensing Agreement or a Sales Agreement. However, as a Sales Agreement, all rights would have been transferred to the buyer for a price. There would have been fewer terms and conditions imposed.

(2) The state of incorporation must be identified, as there is an attempt on the part of different states to prevent the fraudulent purchase or sale of patent rights. For example, Tennessee law makes it a felony (one to five years in the penitentiary) to improperly endorse checks and promissory notes. This is a valid reason for using an attorney from the state of incorporation.

(3) The word "Buyer" could have been substituted in the case of sale.

(4) The date of this Agreement, or the date of agreed effectivity of the Agreement.

(5) This would be modified if joint ownership is involved. Ownership of patent items is subject to later patent issue.

(6) The name used in the patent or patent application or in trademarks or other suitable and descriptive name.

(7) The description of the Invention should be complete in the Inventor's Journal and other documentation, and reference can be made to that documentation.

(8) The numbers are identified and constitute adequate description.

(9) The license is authorization to use the Invention. All manner of limits may be imposed when necessary — geographic or industry or whatever.

(10) Some cash should change hands to confirm the deal. There are no firm guidelines, but reimbursement of Inventor's costs is common. Frequently the amount may be three to five times Inventor's accumulated development costs. The Inventor selling his first invention will be less likely to pull a good amount of this "front money" than his counterpart who has sold many inventions.

(11) The territory can be identified as inclusive or exclusive territory using any desired convenient boundary system. Some boundaries are subject to change as cities grow or rivers meander, so plan accordingly. If non-exclusive territory is assigned, it may be well to tie in the royalty paid by the first Licensee to the royalty charged subsequent Licensees.

(12) Or any other limits. These exceptions, however, may be more trouble than you want to take on in most cases.

(13) If the item is patented, it is usually licensed for the life of the patent. However, it is not uncommon to have an annual payment of money for the life of the Inventor in lieu of royalty accounting. The period of time must be identified in any case.

Footnotes:

(14) The quoted royalty of 5% of the net selling price is not typical of anything in particular. Five percent represents 20% of the profits, before tax, usually realized by a company enjoying an exclusive royalty on a good invention. The amount which is negotiated may well begin with a request for 10%. But if the product is a high-volume, highly-competitive item, 1% or 2% may be generous. If royalty is paid on each unit produced, it is best to tie it to the economy via the consumer price index to allow for inflation.
(15) The use of this term is most acceptable to the Buyer or Licensee. Even though the royalty is a percentage of the profits, computations are difficult, and accounting is subject to definition and separation or records in a manner that is impractical in most cases.
(16) Quarterly payments are very practical because the Federal Government requires quarterly reports.
(17) Records availability means that the office which maintains the accounting will not be so remote that you or your accountant are inconvenienced unnecessarily. You may have to fight for this right and you may never exercise the right, but be firm in your demand for the right.
(18) The Inventor must be reasonable about the setup time before the Licensee can be expected to produce and sell the minimums. The financial size of the company is a consideration. A large company will be able to pay a minimum more readily than a small one.
(19) Minimums may be expressed in dollars or units. If the royalty is a fixed amount on each unit rather than a percentage of the net selling price, the inflation (or deflation) of the economy may seriously affect your income. Inflation will produce a constant erosion of your usable income, and deflation may create an unacceptable profit margin for the Licensee, which may result in problems for the Inventor. Don't kill the goose!
(20) This is 30 days after the end of the reporting period.

Footnotes:

(21) This phrase may be replaced with a whole treatment of quarter-by-quarter or year-by-year minimums. This would permit maximum royalty during peak sales, and as sales of the item fade, reduce royalties in order to encourage continued production.
(22-23) It is important to identify the importance of the Inventor and his continuing role. Try to establish improvements as a basis for renegotiation.

(24) Renegotiation will extend the life of the invention income to the Inventor and encourage the Inventor to continue his participation.
(25) It is desirable to have improvements benefit both parties. It keeps the team together and does not create competition to "get the rascals out." If the Licensee agrees to this, he is indicating that he wants the Inventor to remain involved for their mutual benefit. If the Inventor was valuable at the outset, it makes sense that he will continue to be valuable if rewarded appropriately.
(26) If improvements by the Licensee are not included, the Licensee might have incentive to evolve improvements so as to eliminate the Inventor. Which all too often is the game played by Licensees. It is really a better game for both if there are efforts to maintain rather than sever the relationship.
(27) This is a catchall phrase to include the principles mentioned in the discussion above.

Footnotes:

(28) If the invention is not patented, or if improvements are desirable, or if the Invention has enough potential to warrant a patent application, this should be so identified and responsibility placed in the Agreement.

(29) This phrase may not be suitable for inclusion in your particular case. It refers to copyright and trademarks.

(30) The protection these actions afford the product, when applicable, will help to assure that the Inventor's income from the Invention remains high for a longer period of time.

(31) Marks are required on a patented product, or its packaging, if the product cannot be readily marked, and are desirable on patent-pending products. If a trademark has been associated with a product, it is probably wise to get as much mileage from it as possible by pressing its use.

(32) If a product has been marketed under a trademark, it is possible that the trademark could be more valuable than patents. A separate negotiation could be entered into to sell or license such rights. (The trade name, "Instant Insantiy," overshadowed the value of a patent on the game puzzle, so it was never patented.)

(33) If someone markets a product that is covered by a patent which belongs to another, he is infringing on another's rights.

(34) The cost and responsibility for prosecution must be stipulated. It is usually the Licensee who picks up the tab.

(35) Winnings from action against an infringer. This will cover damages plus royalty for items sold under infringement. The damages should reward the Licensee, and the Inventor should receive royalty normally paid by the Licensee.

(36) As noted in Footnote 35 above.

(37) The shoe is on the other foot.

(38) The Licensee is usually in a far better position financially so the cost of the defense should be his.

(39) It is somewhat true that a patent issued by the Patent Office is not valid until it has withstood the test of a court trial. If a patent is challenged, the court will first make the determinantion that the patent is valid before determining infringement.

(40) If the Licensee loses the exclusive position his Agreement with the Inventor gave him, the incentive for him to pay royalty is of course gone. In effect, the Inventor has nothing to sell, because the court held that (a) someone else — another inventor — was the rightful owner or (b) that the item was in the public domain.

(41) It is frequently to the advantage of the Inventor to permit sublicensing to further expand the sales base.

(42) Granting permission to sublicense would be reckless if it is not spelled out in the Agreement.

(43) It is unlikely that sublicensing to expand sales would not be approved by the Inventor, but it is a safeguard to assure knowledge of the license base.

(44) It is an unfortunate truth that many corporate officials are devoid of conscience in the name of corporate profits, and the Inventor's revenue is a target they frequently attack at the first opportunity.

(Clause XIII is no longer valid due to the Supreme Court decision in Lear v. Adkins case. If the role of the individual inventor is to be restored, this decision will have to be reversed some day. —Mel Fuller).

Footnotes:

Lear v. Adkins was a case in which an individual licensed his gyroscope invention to a corporation. After taking the license, the corporation refused to honor it; it refused to pay the royalties due. Until then it had been the rule that the person or company who benefits under a license is not allowed to attack the validity of the patent. In fact, this is the basic principle of all contract law. But the Supreme Court held that would-be monopolists (e.g., the little inventor, Mr. Adkins, whose contract called for some royalties from Lear, Inc. must be kept in check). In express violation of basic contract law, the licensee was freed to attack the validity of the patent at any time after the license contract was executed irrespective of how valuable the contract had been to the licensee until then. (Note that it had always been the law that the rest of the world, i.e., everyone other than a licensee, is free to attack a patent's validity.) There was no concomitant statement that there is some social good involved in making sure that valid patents owned by small patentees are not litigated so as to legally harass those patentees into bankruptcy by large corporations. No such statement was made and there is no such Supreme Court policy! (From Dr. Irving Kayton's talk on the United States Patent System: Fraud on the Inventor and the Public [And What Can Be Done About It] which he delivered at the National Bureau Conference in Monterey, California, June 11-14, 1973. Dr. Kayton is a Professor of Law and the Director of the Patent Law Program as well as the Computers-in-Law Institute of the George Washington University Law Center in Washington, D.C.)

In our book the Supreme Court decision was in error. At the same conference Jacob Rabinow, who has been Chief of the Office of Invention and Innovation of the National Bureau of Standards since 1972, stated, "I'd like to suggest that patents should be treated differently when they are gotten by corporations as against private investors. A corporate patent, as you have heard several times, is a defensive thing. I believe that IBM does not make money in any real sense on patent royalties. They sell computers. General Motors does not make money on patents, even though they have a great many for various defensive and trade reasons. They sell cars. So a patent to a large corporation is a defensive thing; it's a trade thing; it is not a way of getting money. As a matter of fact, I am told that many of their patent staffs cost more than the royalties they collect, but they are valuable for other reasons, obviously."

(45) It is unlikely that the Inventor will object to transferring rights. However, it is best that he be informed.

(46) This is a simple statement of the survivability of the Agreement.

(47) One of the conditions which can precipitate return of the rights to the Inventor.

(48) Another precautionary condition as above.

(49) Basis for the Inventor to pick up property and move on.

(50) There may have been good reasons for the Licensee not to have made payment. If the reason is good enough, the Inventor does not want to repossess.

(51) Shall not be sold or attached by creditors during bankruptcy.

(52) Another way of saying reposses.

(53) This is an official way of saying "to notify."

(54) It is the responsibility of the Licensee to keep the Inventor informed of any address changes, the responsibility of the Inventor to acknowledge that he has received the change, and vice versa.

(55) This means that the Licensee has not kept his end of the bargain even if the

Footnotes:

breach was an oversight or error.

(56) The Licensee should be granted some period of time to correct his mistakes.

(57) Frequently the services of the Inventor are needed to hasten the development of a marketable product. The Inventor may be the only expert.

(58) The definition of time may be more specific if known or anticipated.

(59) This is a negotiated amount — day, hour, week or other basis.

(60) It is not uncommon for an Inventor to become an employee of the company that finds profit in his abilities.

(61) Or month or other agreed basis.

(62) If the Inventor has established himself as an employee because of his creative contributions, he is also in a position to negotiate for royalty. Once he has established himself, an Inventor is able to negotiate from a position of strength.

(63) Some standard must be established, particularly if payments could be made in foreign currency as Canadian or Australian Dollars.

(64) This is a type of account which holds money until the person withdrawing has been qualified. It also prohibits the depositor from withdrawing, using or attaching.

(65) Under the law, by the Parties of the Agreement, in or out of court, this is an intention expressed to help bring agreement rather than disagreement.

(66) As above, a clarification of the intention.

(67) It is possible that circumstances will develop or exist within the law that voids one of the conditions of the Agreement and it is not the desire to break the contract or to permit it to be broken on such a technicality.

(68) It is nearly impossible to write a contract which covers all conditions. An Agreement is as good as the intention and desire of the participants. Where honest dif-

Footnotes:

ferences of opinions must be resolved, the services of the American Arbitration Association are less expensive than the courts.

(69) A nonprofit organization founded to help arbitrate and resolve differences.

(70) There are certain expenses involved in using the AAA.

(71) Because the costs are reasonable, the Inventor can be treated the same as the Licensee despite their possible differences in financial strength.

(72) The laws of states differ, and the laws by which interpretations are made should be identified. If the Inventor resides in one state and is represented by a lawyer familiar with the laws of that state, and the Licensee and lawyers are from another state, it is important to resolve which state laws will be used to interpret the contract.

(73) This covers communications bearing matters of importance relating to the Agreement.

(74) This is the initial address and will be changed as discussed in Note 54 above.

SUMMARY

That's about the gist of it. Bringing your invention to market has a pretty good chance of success if you follow the instructions laid out in this book. These are tried and true methods that many have used and, through them, reached their goal.

A few last do's and don'ts:

Do have a market in mind before you invent. Even as a book or story or a script has to fit a particular market, so must an invention. To be commercially successful, a book must be read; to be successful, an invention must be sold.

Don't fall in love with your invention. The elimination of useless ideas is as important as the acceptance of good ones. Be as ruthlessly critical when you appraise your idea as you would be in appraising others' ideas.

Do continue to invent. The more you invent, the more you will find to invent for. You will develop an awareness akin to that of the musician who hears fine tonal nuances that those uninitiated to the world of music do not possess.

Do brainstorm your idea. Then let your subconscious take over. Einstein used to solve his equations by taking his conscious mind off the problem — after he had fed all facets of the problem into his subconscious — by taking walks, playing the violin, letting the problem simmer, until suddenly the subconscious delivered the answer — like a computer.

In addition to your own wealth of satisfaction, you are important. Your success will create jobs, wealth, improve the environment, fill social needs or build a healthy economy. You are a special kind of person with a special kind of talent and you play an indispensable role in the advancement of human society.

You can no longer afford to play a lone role but you must unite with others who share this creative talent and make your voice a power to be reckoned with. In the past it has been big business that has used its clout to get laws enacted in its favor. We Inventors must do the same thing. Find an organization with which you are compatible and join with it in fighting for your rights. In union there is strength.

The world is changing. The needs of its inhabitants are in a constant state of flux. We Inventors are creating a whole new generation of business enterprises — a whole new way of life.

Go to it. And good luck. Wherever Inventors Workshop International can help, we will.

SECTION VI

BIBLIOGRAPHY OF BOOKS AND PAMPHLETS RELATING TO INVENTING

The following books, leaflets, pamphlets, magazines, etc. are recommended reading for the inventor. It is suggested that the inventor saturate himself with literature and information on inventors and inventions. The titles marked with an asterisk (*) are available by writing to ILMA Printing & Publishing, P.O. Box 251, Tarzana, CA 91356.

* INVENTORS JOURNAL by Melvin L. Fuller

* INVENTORS TEACH BOARD — A Board Game that teaches the game of inventing by Melvin L. Fuller

* INVENTORS JOURNAL — A Notebook, with instructions, on keeping a diary of inventions.

* COMPLETE GUIDE TO MAKING MONEY WITH YOUR IDEAS AND INVENTIONS by Richard E. Paige

* THE SCIENCE OF CREATING IDEAS FOR INDUSTRY by Richard E. Paige

* LITTLE INVENTIONS THAT MADE BIG MONEY by Richard E. Paige

* PATENTING MANUAL, Second Edition by Alan M. Hale

* TAX BREAKS FOR THE INVENTOR by Anthony L. Andreoli, CPA, with Neal Houlahen, Consultant to Inventors.

* LINES TO REMEMBER by Richard E. Paige

* NIKOLA TESLA — SAVANT GENIUS OF THE 20TH CENTURY by Anthony Shennan

* MAGIC AND FUN OF INVENTING by Paul Brown

* THE NEW ENTREPRENEURS Women Working from Home by Terri P. Tepper and Nona Dawe Tepper

* IEEE TRANSACTIONS ON PROFESSIONAL COMMUNICATIONS

* I THOUGHT OF IT FIRST by R.C. Alexander

* JOJOBA — OIL INVESTMENT OF THE '80s by T.A. Kuepper

* THE MANAGEMENT OF INVENTIVE PEOPLE by Trevor Clark

* NEW PRODUCTS by Noreen Heimbold and Jim Betts

* FAIL SAFE BUSINESS NEGOTIATING STRATEGIES AND TACTICS FOR SUCCESS by Phillip Sperber

* HOW TO DESIGN BETTER PRODUCTS FOR LESS MONEY by A. V. Gunn

* WHAT EVERY ENGINEER SHOULD KNOW ABOUT PATENTS by William G. Konold, Bruce Tittel, Donald F. Frei and David S. Stallard

* WHAT EVERY ENGINEER SHOULD KNOW ABOUT INVENTING by William H. Middendorf

* HOW TO SELL YOUR INVENTION by William E. Reefman

* ORIGINALITY AND INVENTION APPLIED TO LIVELIHOOD AND BUSINESS by Elmer Gates

* HOW TO ASSESS BEFORE YOU INVEST by Gerald G. Udell with Kenneth G. Baker

* THE INCREDIBLE SECRET MONEY MACHINE by Don Lancaster

* MEANS OF CHANGE by Paul Belzer

* HOW TO TURN YOUR IDEAS INTO BIG MONEY by Vernon Brabham, Jr.

* HOW TO BECOME A SUCCESSFUL INVENTOR by Eric P. McNair and James E. Schwenck

* WHAT IS A PATENT? Pamphlet

PRODUCTION FOR THE GRAPHIC DESIGNER; James Craig, Watson-Guptill Publications, NY 1974

THE WAR AGAINST PROGRESS; Herbert L. Meyer, Storm King Publishers, Inc.

HOW TO CASH IN ON YOUR BRIGHT IDEAS; George G. Siposs, Universal Developments Publishing

COPYRIGHT PRIMER; Harry G. Henn, Practicing Law Institute NY

THE SOURCES OF INVENTION; Jewkes, Sawers & Stillerman, St. Martin's Press 1959

THE EMPLOYED INVENTOR IN THE U.S.; Frederick Neumayer and John Stedman, M.I.T. Press 1970

MAVERICK INVENTOR: MY TURBULENT YEARS AT CBS; Peter C. Goldmark, Saturday Review Press/E.P. Dutton

ADVENTURES WITH D.W. GRIFFITH; Karl Brown, Farrar, Straus & Giroux, New York, 1973

BASIC COMPONENTS OF CREATIVITY; Fred Lichtgram

JAPANESE PATENT AND TRADEMARK LAW; Akira Kukimoto, Inside R&D & Technical Insights Inc.

SCIENTIFIC AND TECHNICAL BOOKS AND SERIALS IN PRINT; R. R. Bowker Company, 1979

LIGHTNING IN HIS HAND: THE LIFE STORY OF NIKOLA TESLA; Inez Hunt and Wanetta W. Draper, Omni Publications

PATENT PENDING — HOW TO FILE YOUR OWN PATENT; Wesley J. Haywood and George L. Haywood, Joe Lane Publishing Co., Box 2646 Evergreen, CO 80409

THE GREAT INVENTIONS; Ralph Stein, Ridge Press/Playboy Press

PATENT LAW FUNDAMENTALS; Peter D. Rosenberg, Clark Boardman Company, Ltd.

INVENTION, DISCOVERY AND CREATIVITY: A.D. Moore, New York, Doubleday & Company Inc. 1969

THE POTENTATES: BUSINESS AND BUSINESSMEN IN AMERICAN HISTORY; Ben S. Seligman, New York, The Dial Press 1971

SMALL BUSINESS ADMINISTRATION ANNUAL; S.B.A.

GENERAL INFORMATION CONCERNING PATENTS, Supt. Doc.

QUESTIONS AND ANSWERS ABOUT PATENTS; Supt. Doc.

TRADEMARK RULES OF PRACTICE WITH FORMS AND STATUTES; Supt. Doc.

COPYRIGHT LAWS OF THE UNITED STATES OF AMERICA: Library of Congress

DISCLOSURE DOCUMENT PROGRAM (leaflet), Supt. Doc.

THINK & GROW RICH, Napoleon Hill

CAREERS IN TRADEMARK LAW; U.S. Trademark Association 1977

USE OF ANOTHER'S MARK FOR A COMPONENT IN FINISHED

PRODUCT; COPIES, PARODIES, IN HONEST TRUTH OR UNFAIR COMPETITION, U.S. Trademark Association 1963

WORK OF GADGETS, THE; Tania Grossinger, David McKay Co.

INVENTOR'S PATENT HANDBOOK, Stacy V. Jones, Dial Press

GENERAL INFORMATION CONCERNING PATENTS; All branches of library

GENERAL INFORMATION CONCERNING TRADEMARKS; All branches

GUIDE FOR PATENT DRAFTSMEN: SELECTED RULES; U.S. Patent Office

PATENT LAW FUNDAMENTALS; Peter D. Rosenburg, Clark Boardman Co. Ltd., New York

PUBLIC NEED AND THE ROLE OF THE INVENTOR; Conference on the Public Need and Role of the Inventor, Monterey, CA 1973

INVENTIONS-NECESSITY IS NOT THE MOTHER OF PATENTS RIDICULOUS AND SUBLIME; Stacy V. Jones, Quadrangle, 1973

INVENTING: HOW THE MASTERS DID IT; Byron Michael Vanderbilt, Durham, N.C., Moore Pub. Co., 1974

TRADEMARK PROBLEMS AND HOW TO AVOID THEM; Crain books 1973

HOW EASY TO SEE THE FUTURE: Isaac Asimov

SECTION VII

FORMS

Here are several forms and samples of documents recommended by Inventors Workshop International to help inventors protect their proprietary rights.

In recognizing the tremendous contribution that individual inventors, small businesses and nonprofit organizations make to innovation and the development of new technology, Congress has provided for a 50% subsidy of the new patent fees for "small entities."

In order to take advantage of the reduced patent fees, it will be necessary to fill out a form to claim status as a small entity.

Here, for your convenience, Inventors Workshop International has reprinted three separate forms — one for Inventors, another for Small businesses and a third for Nonprofit Organizations. To qualify, complete one of these forms and attach to your patent application.

Applicant or Patentee: _____

Serial or Patent No.: _____

Filed or Issued: _____

For: _____

Attorney's
Docket No.: _____

VERIFIED STATEMENT (DECLARATION) CLAIMING SMALL ENTITY
STATUS (37 CFR 1.9 (f) and 1.27 (b)) — INDEPENDENT INVENTOR

As a below named inventor, I hereby declare that I qualify as an independent inventor as defined in 37 CFR 1.9 (c) for purposes of paying reduced fees under section 41 (a) and (b) of Title 35, United States Code, to the Patent and Trademark Office with regard to the invention entitled _____
described in

    [ ] the specification filed herewith

    [ ] application serial no. _____ , filed _____ .

    [ ] patent no. _____ , issued _____ .

I have not assigned, granted, conveyed or licensed and am under no obligation under contract or law to assign, grant, convey or license, any rights in the invention to any person who could not be classified as an independent inventor under 37 CFR 1.9 (c) if that person had made the invention, or to any concern which would not qualify as a small business concern under 37 CFR 1.9 (d) or a nonprofit organization under 37 CFR 1.9 (e).

Each person, concern or organization to which I have assigned, granted, conveyed, or licensed or am under an obligation under contract or law to assign, grant, convey, or license any rights in the invention is listed below:

    [ ] no such person, concern, or organization

    [ ] persons, concerns or organizations listed below*

        *NOTE: Separate verified statements are required from each named person, concern or organization having rights to the invention averring to their status as small entities. (37 CFR 1.27)

FULL NAME _____

ADDRESS _____

    [ ] INDIVIDUAL   [ ] SMALL BUSINESS CONCERN   [ ] NONPROFIT ORGANIZATION

FULL NAME _____

ADDRESS _____

    [ ] INDIVIDUAL   [ ] SMALL BUSINESS CONCERN   [ ] NONPROFIT ORGANIZATION

FULL NAME _____

ADDRESS _____

    [ ] INDIVIDUAL   [ ] SMALL BUSINESS CONCERN   [ ] NONPROFIT ORGANIZATION

I acknowledge the duty to file, in this application or patent, notification of any change in status resulting in loss of entitlement to small entity status prior to paying, or at the time of paying, the earliest of the issue fee or any maintenance fee due after the date on which status as a small entity is no longer appropriate. (37 CFR 1.28 (b))

I hereby declare that all statements made herein of my own knowledge are true and that all statements made on information and belief are believed to be true; and further that these statements were made with the knowledge that willful false statements and the like so made are punishable by fine or imprisonment, or both, under section 1001 of Title 18 of the United States Code, and that such willful false statements may jeopardize the validity of the application, any patent issuing thereon, or any patent to which this verified statement is directed.

_____   _____   _____

NAME OF INVENTOR   NAME OF INVENTOR   NAME OF INVENTOR

_____   _____   _____

Signature of Inventor   Signature of Inventor   Signature of Inventor

_____   _____   _____

Date   Date   Date

Applicant or Patentee: _____ Attorney's
Serial or Patent No.: _____ Docket No.: _____
Filed or Issued: _____
For: _____

VERIFIED STATEMENT (DECLARATION) CLAIMING SMALL ENTITY
STATUS (37 CFR 1.9 (f) and 1.27 (c)) — SMALL BUSINESS CONCERN

I hereby declare that I am
   [   ] the owner of the small business concern identified below:
   [   ] an official of the small business concern empowered to act on behalf of the concern identified below:

   NAME OF CONCERN _____
   ADDRESS OF CONCERN _____
_____

I hereby declare that the above identified small business concern qualifies as a small business concern as defined in 13 CFR 121.3-18, and reproduced in 37 CFR 1.9 (d), for purposes of paying reduced fees under section 41(a) and (b) of Title 35, United States Code, in that the number of employees of the concern, including those of its affiliates, does not exceed 500 persons. For purposes of this statement, (1) the number of employees of the business concern is the average over the previous fiscal year of the concern of the persons employed on a full-time, part-time or temporary basis during each of the pay periods of the fiscal year, and (2) concerns are affiliates of each other when either, directly or indirectly, one concern controls or has the power to control the other, or a third party or parties controls or has the power to control both.

I hereby declare that rights under contract or law have been conveyed to and remain with the small business concern identified above with regard to the invention, entitled _____
_____ by inventor(s)
_____ described in

   [   ] the specification filed herewith
   [   ] application serial no. _____ , filed _____ .
   [   ] patent no. _____ , issued _____ .

If the rights held by the above identified small business concern are not exclusive, each individual, concern or organization having rights to the invention is listed below* and no rights to the invention are held by any person, other than the inventor, who could not qualify as a small business concern under 37 CFR 1.9 (d) or by any concern which would not qualify as a small business concern under 37 CFR 1.9 (d) or a nonprofit organization under 37 CFR 1.9 (e).

     *NOTE: Separate verified statements are required from each named person, concern or organization
     having rights to the invention averring to their status as small entities. (37 CFR 1.27)

NAME _____
ADDRESS _____
     [   ] INDIVIDUAL   [   ] SMALL BUSINESS CONCERN   [   ] NONPROFIT ORGANIZATION

NAME _____
ADDRESS _____
     [   ] INDIVIDUAL   [   ] SMALL BUSINESS CONCERN   [   ] NONPROFIT ORGANIZATION

I acknowledge the duty to file, in this application or patent, notification of any change in status resulting in loss of entitlement to small entity status prior to paying, or at the time of paying, the earliest of the issue fee or any maintenance fee due after the date on which status as a small entity is no longer appropriate. (37 CFR 1.28 (b))

I hereby declare that all statements made herein of my own knowledge are true and that all statements made on information and belief are believed to be true; and further that these statements were made with the knowledge that willful false statements and the like so made are punishable by fine or imprisonment, or both, under section 1001 of Title 18 of the United States Code, and that such willful false statements may jeopardize the validity of the application, any patent issuing thereon, or any patent to which this verified statement is directed.

NAME OF PERSON SIGNING _____
TITLE OF PERSON OTHER THAN OWNER _____
ADDRESS OF PERSON SIGNING _____
_____

SIGNATURE _____   DATE _____

Applicant or Patentee: _____ _____ Attorney's
Serial or Patent No.: _____ _____ Docket No.: _____
Filed or Issued: _____
For: _____

VERIFIED STATEMENT (DECLARATION) CLAIMING SMALL ENTITY
STATUS (37 CFR 1.9 (f) and 1.27 (d)) — NONPROFIT ORGANIZATION

I hereby declare that I am an official empowered to act on behalf of the nonprofit organization identified below:

NAME OF ORGANIZATION _____
ADDRESS OF ORGANIZATION _____
_____

TYPE OF ORGANIZATION

[ ] University or other institution of higher education
[ ] Tax exempt under Internal Revenue Service Code (26 USC 501(a) and 501(c) (3))
[ ] Nonprofit scientific or educational under statute of state of The United States of America
     (Name of state _____)
     (Citation of statute _____)
[ ] Would qualify as tax exempt under Internal Revenue Service Code (26 USC 501(a) and 501(c) (3)) if located in
     The United States of America
[ ] Would qualify as nonprofit scientific or educational under statute of state of The United States of America if located
     in The United States of America
     (Name of state _____)
     (Citation of statute _____)

I hereby declare that the nonprofit organization identified above qualifies as a nonprofit organization as defined in 37 CFR
1.9 (e) for purposes of paying reduced fees under section 41(a) and (b) of Title 35, United States Code with regard to the
invention entitled _____ by inventor(s)
_____ described in

[ ] the specification filed herewith
[ ] application serial no. _____ , filed _____ .
[ ] patent no. _____ , issued _____ .

I hereby declare that rights under contract or law have been conveyed to and remain with the nonprofit organization with
regard to the above identified invention.

If the rights held by the nonprofit organization are not exclusive, each individual, concern or organization having rights
to the invention is listed below* and no rights to the invention are held by any person, other than the inventor, who could
not qualify as a small business concern under 37 CFR 1.9 (d) or by any concern which would not qualify as a small business
concern under 37 CFR 1.9 (d) or a nonprofit organization under 37 CFR 1.9 (e).

      *NOTE: Separate verified statements are required from each named person, concern or organization
      having rights to the invention averring to their status as small entities. (37 CFR 1.27)

NAME _____
ADDRESS _____
              [ ] INDIVIDUAL   [ ] SMALL BUSINESS CONCERN   [ ] NONPROFIT ORGANIZATION

NAME _____
ADDRESS _____
              [ ] INDIVIDUAL   [ ] SMALL BUSINESS CONCERN   [ ] NONPROFIT ORGANIZATION

I acknowledge the duty to file, in this application or patent, notification of any change in status resulting in loss of entitlement to small entity status prior to paying, or at the time of paying, the earliest of the issue fee or any maintenance fee
due after the date on which status as a small entity is no longer appropriate. (37 CFR 1.28 (b))

I hereby declare that all statements made herein of my own knowledge are true and that all statements made on information
and belief are believed to be true; and further that these statements were made with the knowledge that willful false statements
and the like so made are punishable by fine or imprisonment, or both, under section 1001 of Title 18 of the United States
Code, and that such willful false statements may jeopardize the validity of the application, any patent issuing thereon, or
any patent to which this verified statement is directed.

NAME OF PERSON SIGNING _____
TITLE IN ORGANIZATION _____
ADDRESS OF PERSON SIGNING _____

SIGNATURE _____ DATE _____

PROTECTION SUMMARY CHART

To Protect	Form or Method	Comments
Conception	Date of Conception Form	This form is, as soon as possible after inspiration, witnessed and notarized. Unecessary if maintaining journal.
Conception	Disclosure Document Program	Filed with the Patent Office (not a Patent Application) - costs $10. Unecessary if maintaining journal.
Invention Construction or Composition	Patent Application	Good for 17 years after granting. May be filed by attorney, agent or inventor.
Invention Appearance	Design Patent	New and ornamental - original. Three-and-a-half, 7 and 14 years and then reverts to public domain.
Invention Appearance	Copyright	Works of art, etc., cheaper than a design patent, not for things of "utility."
Trademark Service Mark Certification Mark Collective	Patent Office Registration and with individual states	Must not be easily confused with another mark or product, nor can it be simply a surname or just a description. This is good forever. Examples abound - Ford, DuPont, Chevrolet, Studebaker, etc.
Package	Patent	A functional construction
Package Design	Design Patent, Registration as Trademark.	The Coca-Cola bottle is a protected shape.
Leaflets	Copyright	

DATE OF CONCEPTION DOCUMENT

Inventor's Name: _____

Inventor's Address: _____

(City)	(State)	(Zip)

This invention was first conceived on (date) _____.

This invention was first described on (date) _____.

Description: _____

_____

_____

_____

_____

_____

_____

_____

Date of first model, if any: _____

This invention description has been read and is understood by the following witnesses:

Name: _____   Name: _____

Address: _____   Address: _____

_____   _____

Inventor's Signature: _____
(To be signed in the presence of Notary Public only)

_____ _____ _____ _____

State of _____ }   On this the _____ day of _____ 19 _____, before

County of _____ } ss   me,

the undersigned Notary Public, personally appeared known to me
to be the person(s) whose name(s) _____ subscribed to the within
instrument and acknowledged that _____ executed the
same for the purposes therein contained.
IN WITNESS WHEREOF, I hereunto set my hand and official seal.

_____
(Signature of Notary Public)

IWI-A (Rev. 1) 6/74

REQUEST FOR ACCEPTANCE OF DISCLOSURE DOCUMENT

COMMISSIONER OF PATENTS AND TRADEMARKS
Washington, D.C. 20231

Sir:

The undersigned, being the inventor of the disclosed invention, requests that the enclosed papers
be accepted under the Disclosure Document Program, and that they be preserved for two years.

Signed _____

Date _____   Name (print) _____

Address _____

_____

Inventor's title and No. of document _____

_____

Enclosed:

    (a) 2 copies of this Request
    (b) 2 copies of Disclosure Document
    (c) 1 stamped self-addressed envelope
    (d) Fee: $10 (Postal money order)

Sample Disclosure Document

John Doe
1234 Elm St.
Pasadena, CA 91106
Disclosure Document #_____

INSTRUMENT FOR ADMINISTERING PILLS TO ANIMALS

It is difficult to administer pills or capsules to dogs, cats, etc. by hand. Veterinarians have long used instruments for "pilling" cows and horses, but few, if any, instruments are available for use with smaller animals.

A suitable instrument should meet the following requirements: 1) one-hand operation; 2) incapable of scratching the animal's mouth or throat; 3) fit pills and capsules over a wide range of sizes and shapes without adjustment; and 4) be simple and cheap, so that veterinarians could supply them to pet owners along with the pills.

Referring to the sketches on page 2, Fig. 1 is a side sectional view of a new instrument of this type. It has a hollow barrel 1 with a flared end 2, all made of soft flexible plastic. Inside the barrel 1 is a rod-shaped plunger 4 which is pushed down to expel the pill 7. A collar 3 and a button 5 provide a way to hold and operate the instrument in the manner of a syringe, pushing the button 5 down with the thumb.

The pill 7 is inserted edgewise into the flared end 2. See the end view of Fig. 2. The pill distorts elastically the barrel end 2 into an elliptical shape. In this way the flared end 2 will take pills of a range of sizes and hold them securely, but not so tightly that they are difficult to push out via the rod 4. Capsules can be inserted endways.

The main features are the softness of the barrel 1 and the flare 2. The barrel 1 need not be stiff enough to stay straight by itself because the plunger rod 4 keeps it straight. In fact, it is better to have the barrel somewhat curved, because it holds the plunger against falling out. Commercial "Tygon" vinyl tubing, 3/16" inside diameter and about 5 inches long has been used successfully. The flare 2 was made with a heated conical mandrel. Parts 3 and 5 were turned from nylon rod stock and cemented on. Rod 4 may be of nylon rod.

Sample Disclosure Document

John Doe
1234 Elm St.
Pasadena, Calif. 91106

Disclosure Document # _____

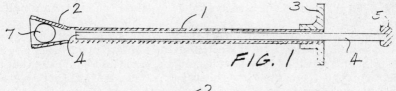

FIG. 1

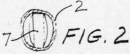

FIG. 2

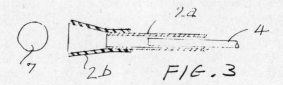

FIG. 3

John Doe

Fig. 3 shows a side section of a modification where the flared end portion 2b is separate from the barrel 2a, and is slipped on and then discarded after use.

John Doe

Page 2

Disclosure

EXPANDED FORM (I.W.I. - B)

THE UNDERSIGNED, BEING THE INVENTOR (S) OF THE DISCLOSED INVENTION,
REQUEST (S) THAT THE ENCLOSED PAPERS BE ACCEPTED UNDER THE DISCLOSURE
DOCUMENT PROGRAM OF THE U.S. PATENT OFFICE, AND THAT THEY BE PRE-
SERVED FOR A PERIOD OF TWO (2) YEARS.

(Please Type or Print):

Inventor's Name: ___Paul_____H._____Comins, Jr.___
　　　　　　　(Full first name)　(Initial)　　(Last name)
Inventor's Address: __19614 Green Mountain Drive_____
　　　　　　__Newhall_____California_____91321___
　　　　　　(City)　　　　　(State)　　　(Zip)

Co-inventors (if any):
(1) __None_____ (2) __None_____

　　(Mailing Address)　　　　　　(Mailing Address)

　(City, State & Zip Code)　　　(City, State & Zip Code)

The INVENTION is called: __Blade Handle Assembly__
The INVENTION'S __January 18, 1974_____January 18, 1974___
　　　(Date of Conception)　　(Date of First Description-Sketch)

Paul H Comins jr　　　　　_Jan 18, 1974_
　　　　　(ure)

State of _CALIFORNIA_　　Mary B Smith　(3) _____ 19__, before me,
County of _LOS ANGELES_ }ss. (Signature)
　　　　　　　　　(Address)　　lly appeared

SAMPLE

known to be the person whose name(s) _is_ subscribed
the within instrument and acknowledged that __he__
executed the same for the purposes therein contained.
IN WITNESS WHEREOF, I hereunto set my hand and official seal.

OFFICIAL SEAL
PAUL H. COMINS, JR.
NOTARY PUBLIC-CALIFORNIA
LOS ANGELES COUNTY
My Commission Expires Aug. 29, 1976

SIGNATURE, JURISDICTION, EXPIRATION DATE AND ADDRESS OF NOTARY PUBLIC

115

DRAWING OR SKETCH:

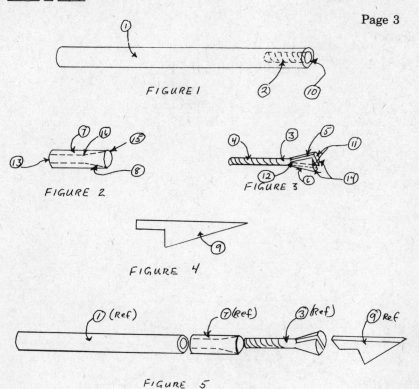

FIGURE I

FIGURE 2

FIGURE 3

FIGURE 4

FIGURE 5

DESCRIPTION:

The handle device assembly will consist of four prime parts: Figure 1, the handle (1); Figure 2, the sleeve (7); Figure 3, the vice grip (3); and Figure 4, the blade (9). The handle (1) is to be drilled (10) and tapped (2) in one end. The vice grip (3) is threaded on one end (4) to fit the tapped hole (10) in the handle. The vice grip will have a tapered portion (6) which extends from the threads to the face (11). The vice grip face (11) has a slit (5) which forms the jaws (14) into which a blade (9) can be inserted. This slit (5) extends into the vice grip to point (12). The sleeve (7) is to be tubular with its smallest inside diameter (13) larger than the diameter of the threads of Item 3. From point (16) to point (15) this hold is to be tapered to approximate the taper (6) on the vice grip. The handle assembly is assembled as shown in Figure 5. The sleeve (7) is used to add support and to tighten the jaws (14) of the vice grip.

MATERIALS:

The handle (1), sleeve (7), and the vice grip (3) to be made of brass, aluminum or similar material. The blade (9) will be of steel or other substance capable of being sharpened to a cutting edge.

HOW TO FILE THIS DISCLOSURE DOCUMENT UNDER THE 1969 PATENT OFFICE DISCLOSURE DOCUMENT PROGRAM

GENERAL INFORMATION: **THIS IS NOT A PATENT APPLICATION.**

Through the U.S. Patent Office, this new service provides for inventors the acceptance and preservation for a period of two (2) years this evidence of the date of conception of this invention. The Document may be forwarded to the Patent Office by the inventor, inventors (or by anyone of the inventors when there are joint inventors), owners, or by the attorney or agent of the inventor(s) or owner.

It will be destroyed after two years unless it is referred to in a related patent application within the two year period. The date of receipt in the Patent Office will not become the effective filing date of any patent application subsequently filed. However, like patent applications, this document will be kept in confidence by the Patent Office.

The value of the conventional witnessed and notarized records as evidence of conception of an invention is not hereby diminished in any way. There are no restrictions as to content. Claims need not be made. However, the benefits afforded by this Disclosure Document will depend directly upon its adequacy. It is therefore, strongly urged that this document contain a clear and complete explanation of the manner and process of making and using the invention in sufficient detail to enable a person having ordinary knowledge in the field of the invention to make and use the invention.

Be sure to use the space allocated for a sketch, drawing, or photograph (if the nature of the invention permits), and always describe the use or utility, especially in chemical inventions.

WARNING: The two year retention period should not be considered to be a "grace period" during which the inventor can wait to file his patent application without possible loss of benefits. It must be recognized that in establishing priority of invention an affidavit or testimony referring to a Disclosure Document must usually also establish diligence in completing the invention or in filing patent application after the filing of this Document.

Inventors are also reminded that any public use or sale in the United States or publications of the invention anywhere in the world more than one year prior to the filing of a patent application on that invention will prohibit the granting of a patent on it.

DIRECTIONS FOR COMPLETING THIS FORM AND FILING WITH PATENT OFFICE: A FEE of $10.00 is charged by the Patent Office for this service. Payment must accompany the Disclosure Document when it is submitted to the Patent Office. If a check or money order is used, it should be made payable to "Commissioner of Patents." Mail it with the Disclosure Document to: Comissioner of Patents, Washington, D.C. 20231.

In addition to the FEE, the Disclosure Document must be accompanied by a stamped, self-addressed envelope and a duplicate of this Disclosure. The papers will be stamped by the Patent Office with an identifying number and date of receipt, and the duplicate will be returned in the self-addressed envelope together with a notice indicating that the Disclosure Document may be relied upon only as evidence and that a patent application should be diligently filed if patent protection is desired.

THIS INFORMATION WAS FURNISHED BY THE U. S. PATENT OFFICE.

The following is a suggested form to be signed by the representative of a company when an invention is presented to that company for evaluation and possible licensing or purchase.

CONFIDENTIAL DISCLOSURE AGREEMENT

I, _____, authorized to act and sign on behalf of

_____, do hereby, for and on behalf of the said company, agree to receive in confidence an invention known as_____

_____. Said invention will be evaluated by _____

_____ (company) for interest in further negotiations as a product or idea to be produced and/or marketed by said company.

I further agree that said company will not use, sell, assign, disclose, or in any manner utilize for profitable gain the said suggestion, invention/idea disclosed by you, except as may be by mutual agreement, separately concluded between us.

We assume no responsibility and accept no liability regarding features which can be demonstrated to be already know to me or us, or that may become known to me or us in the future on an unrestricted basis through legal channels from a source not covered by an agreement with the Inventor similar to this, and where we didn't directly or indirectly initiate the transmission of such information from the Inventor to us.

We will review the subject matter to be received from you and inform you within forty-five (45) days of the results of our findings, and whether or not we are interested in contracting with you for rights to use the suggestion, invention/idea.

By_____

Date _____

MARKET RESEARCHING — IN A NUT SHELL

Market Research is required by the inventor to determine the barriers to successfully introducing his new product into the marketplace.

I. The following brief instructions are aimed at helping the Inventor to develop a set of survey questions that will provide a better view of the chances of success of a product in the marketplace. It is only one of the tools needed, and the results are not absolute — but nonetheless essential. The purpose of a survey is to determine:

    A. If a product is wanted.
    If it will be used.
    If it will be acceptable — or treasured.
    B. If someone will want someone else to have the product.

II. The essence of the data required is found in the answers to the following questions:
    1. Do you think there is a place in the market for this product?
    2. What do you like most about it?
    3. What do you like least about it?
    4. At what retail price should it be sold?
    5. If it is sold at the price you indicate, would you like to order one or be notified of its availability?
    6. Name and address.
    7. Qualifier questions, i.e., age, sex, occupation, experience, etc.

III. The inventor/surveyor —
    A. The inventor drops his role as inventor and becomes the survey taker. He wants and needs honest answers — not an ego trip.
    B. The "like most" and "like least" responses must be taken down verbatim and will become sales and promotion phrases in future advertising and user literature. Get it all down. People being interviewed will be more spontaneous while talking than while writing.
    C. It will be helpful if you tell them you will provide them with a summary — and later do it!!

IV. How Much Is Enough?
    The following is an example of the bell curve that will result from staticizing the result of the market research. The greates number of responses in any given price range WILL DETERMINE THE FINAL RETAIL PRICE OF THE PRODUCT. For this illustrative example we have surveyed 50 people. The distribution of the price responses are shown in the

chart below. This clearly shows that the selling price for this product must be pegged at $3.99 to $4.00. All of your test results won't be as idealized as this, but it is important to run enough surveys to find the "Bell" and to get all of the important "Like Most" and "Like Least" answers.

If the consumer values your product at a price less than your cost plus profit, you either have to redesign to reduce cost or profit or abandon the whole project. Your complete marketing strategy depends on answers you'll get from this survey.

Questions to consumer: At what price do you think this product should retail? ($1-2) ($2-3) ($3-4) ($4-5) ($5-6). More? Or less? You will get specific numbers and not just vague answers.

```
                                        X
                                        X
                                        X
                                        X
                                        X
                                        X
                                        X
                                        X
                                        X
                                        X           X
                                        X           X
                            X           X           X
                            X           X           X
                            X           X           X
                            X           X           X
                  X         X           X           X
                  X         X           X           X
    X       X     X         X           X           X       X
    X       X     X         X           X           X       X       X
    X       X     X         X           X           X       X       X
  Less    $1-$2 $2-$3     $3-$4       $4-$5       $5-$6     $6-$7    More
  than                                                              than
  $1                                                                $7
```

1. If your cost (production, labor and materials) is $1.00, this curve shows a 5 times markup, and you can utilize all conventional methods of marketing.

2. If your cost is $1.60, this curve shows only a 3 times markup, and you will be able to sell to retailers who sell to consumers — but not through jobbers, distributors and other middlemen.

3. If your cost is $2.50, this curve shows a 2 time markup, and must sell direct from factory to consumer.

PATENTS, DESIGN PATENTS, AND TRADEMARKS ISSUED 1965-1982

This is a list of patent, design patent and trademark numbers that have been issued in the past 17 years. Design patents expire in 14 years (maximum) but trademarks are strengthened with use, although they must be renewed every 20 years.

Year	17 Years Patent	Up to 14 Years Design	20 Years Trademark
1965	3,226,728	203,378	801,120
1966	3,295,142	206,566	821,386
1967	3,360,799	209,731	841,432
1968	3,419,906	213,083	862,960
1969	3,487,469	216,418	883,573
1970	3,551,908	219,636	905,318
1971	3,631,538	222,792	926,339
1972	3,707,728	225,694	949,593
1973	3,781,913	229,728	975,708
1974	3,858,240	234,031	1,000,861
1975	3,930,270	238,314	1,029,019
1976	4,000,519	242,880	1,055,347
1977	4,065,811	246,810	1,080,672
1978	4,131,951	250,675	1,110,302
1979	4,180,866	253,795	1,128,463
1980	4,242,756	257,745	1,145,373
1981	4,308,621	262,494	1,184,280
1982	4,366,578	267,439	1,221,984

SECTION VIII

PATENT LANGUAGE

Introduction

I. The Language

To businessmen, researchers, students and others who have occasion to read in the U.S. patent literature or to deal with the patent profession, patents may appear to be written in a kind of English gone slightly awry, and the business of dealing with the Patent and Trademark Office to be complex (which it is). To the professional, the language and the procedures seem natural. This glossary attempts to bridge the gap.

In undertaking this, it has to explain and describe a number of institutions, practices and concepts that are peculiar to the field. Some of the ideas are not obvious at a glance. For example, the principle behind claims is no simpler than that behind short selling, or puts and calls.

This is a dictionary of usage as well as terms, and so includes words and phrases that are employed only in special senses, and other terms that are, by rule or custom, in effect forbidden. Some of the entries are what might be called procedural terms, such as "specification," "claim," "allow," "reject," "amendment," "enter." Most of these are used in one sense only and have no synonyms, in a way similar to the usage of the terms "factor," "product," "integrate" in mathematics.

Certain common words that might appear offhand to be synonyms for procedural terms, such as "disallow" for "reject," are listed as being avoided. Another category of entries is the terms that are used about their usual meanings, but are strongly preferred over any ordinary synonyms, such as "comprising," "provide," "substantially."

The words of a language can be defined only in terms of each other. This is true of a sub-language too, to a noticeable extent. It is not feasible to define "rejection" without using "claim" and "action." Each term needing it is defined once in ordinary English, but is also used where necessary in the definitions of other terms.

The recorded literature involved is extensive. Assuming an average of 2500 words per patent and not counting the illustrations, the whole "file" of four-million-odd U.S. patents amounts to 10 billion words.

The definitions given are based on the standard authorities where any exist, but they were written by me, and no one else is responsible. Notice of errors and omissions will be gratefully received.

The entries are confined to those special words and expressions common in the writing of applications for U.S. patents, and in the Patent Office practice and related matters. Legal terms not common in patent practice are excluded.

II. Patents as technological literature

As a reference library of technology, the natural collection or "file" of over four million U.S. patents is a unique resource. Per page, the idea content is high. By definition every one is different. Manufacturers and professional inventors often maintain reference collections of patents on their particular subjects. The national "file" is not, however, used nearly as much as regular libraries. One reason is that there are only two complete sets in the country that are classified and arranged by subject, one at the Public Search Room of the Patent Office and the other at the public library in Sunnyvale, California. (West Germany has 20). About 20 libraries in America have sets of patents arranged in numerical order, but these are of very limited use, like a random collection of books.

Another reason may be the style and format peculiar to patents and the enormous variety of subjects. Some discussion of this may be useful. Patents are written to facilitate skimming, and the drawing is used as a framework. Typically, one scans the drawing for some telltale feature, notes the number applied to it, then looks for that number in the Detailed Description section. Drawing figures are not arranged orthogonally. The short section beginning "in the Drawing" tells what the views are.

Verbal fluency is a special aptitude unrelated to other kinds of thinking. The text of a patent is rarely as readable as a magazine article. The anticipated readership is small and the real objective is legal. Trade and technical magazine articles, on the other hand, are often inhibited by considerations of commercial secrecy and the need to sell the products of advertisers. Engineering textbooks tend to shun the practical.

Patents are required to be practical. The full disclosure rule is strict, and the trend of court decisions has been to interpret it stricktly. A patentee who holds out important information runs the risk of having a court hold the patent invalid.

With some exceptions, anything patented is, or was, hoped by someone to make money in the commercial market. Most never made it. The patent literature is full of intermediate inventions, runners-up. When the best way to get some result is found, it supersedes its predecessors. Not uncommonly, however, an old runnerup is made more feasible by some new background technology (such as microprocessors), and the old idea takes on a new life. Some arts such as geometrical optics and applied mechanics go on steadily almost from century to century. Huge and veriegated as the "file" of four million is, there is no safe way to declare this or that item, or group, obsolete.

The writer of a patent application is necessarily concerned with degrees of specificity and degrees of generality. Common terms of patent language as "comprise," "generally," "means," "prior" reflect this concern. Synonyms are usually avoided, the same word being used to mean the same thing. Often it is necessary to devise ad hoc names for certain parts of a thing described; frequently for reasons of safety, a couple of names are coined ("...a corner post or column...") and defined early in the text, then one or both used in what follows.

***

ABANDON   Of an invention, to give it up or dedicate it to the public, either expressly or by making it public and then failing to file a patent application within the 1-year limit. See *Statutory Bar*.

Of a patent application, to kill it or to permit it to die. The Patent Office holds an application *abandoned*, e.g., for failure to *respond* to an Office *action* within the time limit set, or for failure to pay the issue fee in time. Other reasons for a holding of abandonment occur in more complicated circumstances. Abandoned applications are sent to the *Abandoned Files* and left there. Not being published, they cannot be cited against other applications as *prior art*. They are not open to the public, but may be made available to parties in interest in certain circumstances. Procedural occasions occur, e.g., in *continuations* when it is advisable to *expressly abandon* an application. One can file a *petition to revive* a case held abandoned, but the petition must show that any delay, e.g., in responding, was unavoidable.

ABBREVIATIONS, COMMON

⎯⎯   allowed (of a claim or of a whole application)

appln.   application for a patent

C.D.   Decisions of the Commissioners of Patents, vol. pub. annually by Govt. Printing Office 1870-1968

CCPA   U.S. Court of Customs and Patent Appeals (Wash., D.C.)

CFR   Code of Federal Regulations

CIP   Continuation-in-Part (application)

cl.   claim, class

exr.   examiner (patent)

J.   judge (in printed decisions)

MPEP   Manual of Patent Examining Procedure

obj.   objection, objected to

O.G.   Official Gazette of the U.S. Patent Office

P.J.   presiding judge (in printed decisions)

PO   Patent Office (now PTO)

pre-ex   preliminary search

PTO   Patent and Trademark Office

R., rej.   rejected, rejection

S.N.   Serial Number (of a patent application)

spec.   specification, of a patent or an application

sub   subclass

U.S.C.   United States Code (statutes)

USPQ   U.S. Patents Quarterly (jour. of legal decisions, pub. by Bureau of National Affairs, Inc.)

uxr   unofficial cross-reference (in examiners' search files)

WIPO   World Intellectual Property Organization (Geneva)

xr   cross-reference (pat. classification for search, etc.)

÷   division (of a patent or application)

ABSTRACT   "A concise statement of the technical disclosure of a patent" (MPEP). Required at the beginning of an application since 1965. Currently limited to 1 paragraph and 250 words. Not to be interpreted as limiting the claims, hence should be written in straight technical English, without hedging.

ACCORDING TO THE INVENTION In a *specification*, a phrase used to identify something that is considered a part of the invention, in contrast to something that is not. Fairly often needed, since an invention is embedded in its technological surroundings. See *known*.

ACTION An official letter from an *Examiner* to an *applicant* stating, e.g., any of the following: (1) *references cited*; (2) *claims allowed* or *rejected*; (3) requirements for *restriction*; (4) *objections* to parts of application; (5) making a previous action *final*. Syn., *Office letter*. Always includes a *period for response*. Reasons for rejecting claims must be given; reasons for allowance are not usually given. The language is normally brief and standardized. *Forms* are used liberally. Usually written by an *assistant Examiner* and signed by a *primary Examiner*. No relation to the term *action* in general law.

ACTION, SUPPLEMENTAL An *action* following another action when no *amendment* has intervened, to correct an error or to cite a newly-found *reference*. Relatively uncommon.

ADVANCE THE PROSECUTION To move a *case* closer to its final disposition, i.e., *allowance* or *abandonment*, as by reducing the number of issues under consideration and defining them more clearly. An issue once determined, one way or the other, may not be reopened (otherwise, you wouldn't get anywhere). The *Remarks* in an *amendment* sometimes say that a certain move was made to advance the prosecution of the case when it appears to the examiner that it does not. Every action and amendment is supposed to advance the prosecution.

AGENT, PATENT A registered patent practitioner who is not also a lawyer. See *Registration*.

AGGREGATION In a *claim*, a collection of elements which do not cooperate to produce any new and unobvious result, but operate each in their usual ways, e.g., a pocket-knife with a screwdriver blade, scissors, etc. A ground for rejection. The opposite of *combination*. Not too common nowadays.

ALLOWANCE By an *examiner* or higher authority, a formal ruling that a *claim* or claims, or a whole application (i.e., all the *claims* then in it) are patentable, and will be part of the patent when it issues.

ALTERNATIVE EXPRESSION Generally forbidden in U.S. *claims* as *vague* and *indefinite* language, e.g., "a screw or a rivet". A generic word would be required instead, e.g., "a fastener". *Either, or, any, some of*, are among the terms avoided. See *Markush group, vague*. There are exceptions. Usage tends to grow more liberal.

AMENDED CLAIM A *claim* whose wording has been changed according to the directions given in an *amendment*. No more than 5 words may be inserted in a *claim* by an *amendment* which simply directs the cancellation or insertion of words in specified lines. If more than 5 words are to be inserted, the whole claim must be submitted in rewritten form with the insertions underlined and the deletions in brackets (Rule 121). Or, the claim may be cancelled and a new claim submitted in its place. See *fees, amendment*.

AMENDMENT Vital part of the *prosecution* of a *patent application*. Usually, a document filed directing specified changes in the *specification* and/or *claims* of an application in response to an *Office action*. Concludes with a section "Remarks", submitting appropriate explanation, summarization, argument, etc. The response to an *action* is typically in the form of an amendment. It may, e.g., cancel, add, and/or amend claims, and correct typographical errors. Under *Remarks* is typically a detailed discussion of the invention, action, references, claims, and the relationships between them, with a detailed argument designed to show why the claims as amended are believed to be allowable. Typically, an amendment is considerably longer than the *action* to which it responds. The amendment must meet every ground of *objection* and *rejection* given in the *action*; else it may be held to be *not responsive*. An amendment may be filed after filing an application but not before the first action; but matter disclosed in it will not get the benefit of the filing date of the application itself, but only of the date of the amendment. *New matter* (which see) will not be *entered*.

An amendment may be submitted after a *final rejection* and may be entered, but not as a matter of right unless all it does is to cancel all the rejected claims and comply with any standing

INVENTORS GUIDEBOOK

formal requirements. See *rejection, final; enter; supplemental.* Where appropriate, an amendment may contain only, e.g. *Remarks.*

AMENDMENT, PRELIMINARY   An amendment filed before the first Office action, as for the purpose of adding *claims* or correcting typographical errors. *New matter* is not permitted. See *new matter.*

AMENDMENT, SUPPLEMENTAL   *Amendment* filed after another amendment when there has been no intervening *action on the merits.* May be in response to a notice of some *formal* defect in the preceding amendment, such as directions to insert more than 5 words in a claim.

ANTECEDENT   In a *claim,* the first appearance of an element which also appears later, the later appearance being typically preceded by the word "said." If a "said" element appears in a claim without an antecedent, the examiner will *object* to the claim.
   Ex.:
   In a claim saying: An engine having a camshaft, and means to drive said camshaft, said timing chain having . . .

the term "timing chain" has no antecedent. To overcome the inevitable objection, that part of the claim might be reworded:
   Ex.:
   An engine having a camshaft, and a timing chain driving said camshaft, said timing chain having . . .

In a *dependent* claim, antecedents may be in the *parent claim.*

ANTICIPATION   A showing that an alleged invention, or some part of it, is *old,* by disclosing it under a prior publication date. A showing in, say, a 1966 patent or published article may *anticipate* claims in a 1976 application. See *old.*

ANY   One of the words avoided in *claims* as being *indefinite* or *alternative.* In a sense, the article *a* as ordinarily used in claims means *any;* this does not affect the usage.

APPARATUS CLAIM   A *claim* directed to the apparatus used in practicing an invention, as contrasted to the method or process of the invention (if it has one). See *restriction, division.*

APPEAL   Applicants have the right to appeal from a *final rejection* by an *examiner* to the Board of Patent Appeals of the Patent and Trademark Office, and from an adverse decision by the Board to the U. S. Court of Customs and Patent Appeals (CCPA) or to the U. S. Court of Appeals for the District of Columbia. In an appeal to the Board, the steps involve (1) filing a Notice of Appeal (a simple form) with a $50 fee, and (2) filing an Appeal Brief within 2 months after (1) with another $50 fee. An oral hearing in Washington may be requested and often is, even, it is said, when the *attorney* or *agent* intends to cancel it later. After the Examiner gets the Appeal Brief, he must prepare an *Examiner's Answer,* a copy of which is then furnished the applicant. Rare procedural situations occur when the only way to gain time for other purposes after a *final rejection* is to file a Notice of Appeal, after which the appeal may be dropped. Final rejections and certain other matters are appealable; certain others are not, but may be the subject of a *Petition to the Commissioner.* A complex subject. Specifics given in *MPEP.*

APPEALS, BOARD OF   Board of 15 *Examiners-in-Chief* who specialize in hearing appeals. Three members hear each case, and are generally selected as having technical familiarity with the subject of the case on appeal.

APPEAL BRIEF   Brief due within two months after filing a Notice of Appeal to the Board of Appeals. Must contain (1) a "clean copy" of the claims on appeal, (2) concise description of the invention, complete enough so that the original specification need not be read in detail, (3) appropriate discussion of the final rejection and references, statement of the applicant's position, and the necessary explanations and arguments, (4) copies of the relevant references, etc. If the brief is not filed in time, the appeal is automatically dismissed and the case may become *abandoned* (depending on other factors). A $50 fee must accompany the brief. An appeal brief in a

128

simple case may run to perhaps 5-15 pages; in a complicated case considerably more. A published Board decision has criticized a 50-page appeal brief as unnecessarily long.

APPEAL, NOTICE OF   One-page document which identifies an application and says, "Applicant hereby appeals to the Board of Appeals. . . from the final rejection of. . . by the Examiner," etc. Must be accompanied by (currently) a $50 fee, and must be filed within the period for response set in the Final Rejection which is being appealed from. See *Appeal Brief.*

APPELLANT   In an appeal to the Board of Appeals or to a court, the party who does the appealing. Corresponds approximately to a plaintiff.

APPELLEE   In appeal to a court, the party opposite to the appellant, corresponding generally to the defendant. In the Office, an appeal to the Board is *ex parte,* i.e., there is no named appellee. If however the case is further appealed to a court, it automatically becomes an *inter partes* case, and the Commissioner is named as appellee. He is represented in court by a lawyer from the Office of the Solicitor 'of the Office.

APPLICANT   The party applying for a patent. In the U.S., the inventor or inventors. In various other countries the applicant may be the owner of the application, e.g., an employer. There are no age or citizenship requirements. The applicant is nominally the party speaking; e.g., an *amendment* is often signed:

JOHN DOE
applicant

by_____
his attorney or agent

Documents are customarily written in the third person, e.g., "Applicant respectfully disagrees. . . ." In this book, the term *applicant* is used, where convenient, interchangeably with *attorney* or *agent.*

APPLICATION   For a patent, a typed description of an invention with a drawing, a set of claims, and a signed petition and declaration (or oath) form, all made up according to the Rules of Practice and mailed to the Commissioner of Patents and Trademarks with a check for the required filing fee. If and when the patent issues, its text will be the same as that of the application as amended, minus the petition, etc. form. Roughly two-thirds of the applications filed become patents. The rest *go abandoned.*

ARCUATE   In the general shape or nature of an arc of a circle. A more specific term than "curved;" often used in patent applications, particularly in claims, to denote the shape of a mechanical or structural part, a path of motion, etc.

ARRANGE, ARRANGEMENT   Terms frowned on, particularly in *claims,* as carrying some connotation of *obviousness.* See *obvious, dispose.* "Arrange" is considered more restrictive than *dispose,* which is widely used in this general sense.

ART   Any definable branch or area of science or technology; any class of technological information or knowledge. The *Manual of Classification* is sometimes used as the authority as to what are separate *arts* in disputes with applicants over requirements for *division* or *restriction.* An *art* may be, e.g., that of polymer chemistry, textile machinery, magnetic recording. See *state of the art; art, prior.*

ART, PRIOR   The whole body of previously *published* or publicly available information, anywhere in the world, about an *art,* or pertinent to the alleged invention described in an application. What an Examiner searches, or an inventor or other searcher making a preliminary search before filing an application. In the Patent and Trademark Office, the Public Search Room contains only U.S. patents. The examiners' search files also include selected copies of foreign patents and technical publications, but U.S. patents predominate. It is OK to walk into the rooms of an examining group and ask to search in their *art,* on the understanding that you take no more than a few minutes of an examiner's time and put things back before you leave. This is common practice with Washington, D.C. searchers. It is also assumed or hoped that you understand what you are looking for. It is not too usual, however, for *prior art* to be found in the examining groups that is notably closer than that available in the Public Search Room, although often an examiner's *unofficial subclass* has a more up-to-date definition than the nearest official subclass.

The Design Group uses extensive collections of illustrated commercial catalogs, such as Sears. See *classification, design, publication, search.*

ASSIGNEE   The party acquiring a patent or an application by assignment; an owner who is not the inventor or inventors. Most often, an assignee is the corporate employer of a *captive inventor.*

ASSIGNMENT   A transfer of ownership of an application or of a patent, i.e., a gift or sale. Generally speaking, assignments are recorded in the Patent Office. Current recording fee is $20.

ASSIGNOR   The party making an assignment; the giver or seller.

ASSOCIATE   A patent attorney or agent, usually with offices in the Washington, D.C. area, appointed by the principal attorney or agent in a case. Often appointed on an ad hoc basis to handle, e.g., an interview with an *Examiner.*

ATTORNEY, PATENT   A person registered to practice before the Patent Office who is also a lawyer. See *registration.* Non-lawyers registered before 1938 are also called patent attorneys; if registered after that time, patent agents. The term *agent* is usual in most foreign countries.

AVOID   Of a *claim*, to define something patentable over what is shown in a *reference.* If a claim *patentably avoids* a reference, it is *allowable* over that reference.

BOILER PLATE (colloq.)   Business term, particularly in the field of Government contracting. Not used in patent practice, but frequently used in contracts.

BACKGROUND OF THE INVENTION   A section in the specification of an application or patent. See *specification.*

BAR, STATUTORY   See *statutory bar.*

BASE CLAIM   An independent claim, parent to other *dependent claims.* See *claim.*

BEST MODE   A patent application is required to include a description of the "best mode" of applying the inventive concept of which the inventor knows at the time if filing. He can also include other examples. The requirement is enforced most strongly in chemical cases. The reason: The best form of a mechanical device is typically pretty well apparent once the principle is clear; but in chemistry it is not normally apparent which of a variety of related "recipes" is going to work best. If the application describes only the second-best mode, the owner could practice the best one without making it public — in effect getting around the basic principle of patent laws, that the thing patented must be open to the public, not secret.

BOARD OF APPEALS   See *appeal.*

BRANCH   Term used for certain clerical parts of the Patent Office organization, e.g., *application branch, mail branch.*

BREADTH   Of a claim, the extent of the range of equivalents that would infringe it; the size of the outer boundaries of its coverage, in a qualitative or relative sense. See *claim.*

BRIEF   See *appeal brief. Briefs on motions* are part of *interference* practice. The term does not arise in ordinary *prosecution* of a case before the Examiner.

BRIEF SUMMARY OF THE INVENTION   A section of a *specification.*

BUSINESS, METHOD OF DOING   Outside of the statutory class of patentable subject matter. In practice, secrecy or obfuscation are often used in lieu of patents.

130

CANCEL Of a claim, to remove, strike out. Can only be done by direction of the applicant. When an *amendment* directs the cancellation of a claim or claims, its "Remarks" section does not usually give any reasons, except perhaps to say that it was done to *advance the prosecution* of the case, or to better define the invention.

CAPTIVE COUNSEL (colloq.) An attorney employed full-time by an industrial or governmental employer and not free to take outside cases.

CAPTIVE INVENTOR (colloq.) Inventor who has agreed in writing to *assign* all his inventions, or all in some category, to his employer. In some common types of compulsory employer-employee agreements in the U.S., the consideration that the employer pays in return for the invention is one dollar. Often the dollar is not paid, the employee being merely required to sign an assignment which contains the words, "receipt of which is hereby acknowledged." Sometimes he gets a standard honorarium of, say $25-$100.

CASE An application for a patent; everything in its Patent Office file. Often used interchangeably with *application*.

CHARACTERIZED BY Term and style used in German and certain other foreign *claims*, not U.S.

> Ex.:
> A process for refining aluminum from ore, characterized by the electrolysis of bauxite mixed with cryolite . . .

Important in foreign practice.

CITE Said of *references* and of decisions. To list a prior patent, publication, or decision as being pertinent to the matter at hand. In his first *action*, an *Examiner cites references* by listing them on a form, enclosing copies. Typically, 2 to 8 U.S. patents may be cited, and fairly often a foreign patent or an extract from a technical book or article. The references that he cites are those that he officially considers to come closest to showing the same thing as the alleged invention claimed in the application. Decisions of courts, Boards of Appeal, and Commissioners may also be *cited* as authority for some action, position, or ruling by an Examiner, or by an attorney or agent as authority for *his* position. Decisions are not cited nearly as often in Office practice as they are in general law.

CLAIM One of the most important parts of a patent or an application. One of the numbered paragraphs at the end of the document, which define formally what would infringe the patent. Anything infringing a claim must have all the *elements (items)* listed in the claim . It may have more. But if it has fewer, it would not infringe. A short claim containing only a few elements is likely to be *broad,* and hence difficult to avoid infringing; hence desirable. A long, detailed claim is likely to be *narrow,* hence in a sense, less desirable. Claims define in words the boundaries of the patent's *monopoly,* and are the main subject of the proceedings between the applicant and the Patent Office. The applicant normally tries to get allowance of the *broadest* claims that he thinks he is entitled to. A complex subject on which treatises are published, and courses taught. Except in *design* cases, it is customary to submit a set of several claims in an application, graded from *broad* to *narrow.* The broader may get *rejected* and the narrower *allowed.* In an infringement suit, a court may hold certain broader claims invalid, and some narrower claims valid. Without the narrower, more *specific* claims, there would be nothing left. Without the broader claims, the scope of the patent would be unnecessarily restricted. In claims, specially defined terms are sometimes needed. These should be defined in the *specification;* the definitions will hold. See *element, limitation, broad, specific.* An unduly broad claim, even if allowed by the Office, may not be *valid.* A well-written specific claim may be valuable in an infringement suit.

CLAIM, DEPENDENT A claim which refers to another claim, and by so doing automatically includes all the *limitations* and *elements* of that claim.

> Ex.:
> Say an independent claim 1 has elements A, B, C, and D, and a dependent claim 2 reads:

2. The combination of claim 1, further comprising an E and an F.

Claim 2 automatically includes A, B, C, D, E, and F. See *in extenso*. The introductory clause of a dependent claim may be worded variously; all have the same effect: "An X as in claim 1, further comprising . . .", the Y of claim 9, wherein . . ." Before 1965, most claims were independent in form, although this made for more work all around. In 1965, preferential fees were prescribed which favored the use of dependent claims. Currently, the majority of claims are dependent, as they are in foreign practice.

Multiply-dependent claims were first permitted in 1978 by a rule change made to agree with the *Patent Cooperation Treaty*. Such a claim refers to either of two other claims, e.g., "A machine as in claims 2 or 3, further comprising. . . ."

CLAIM, INDEPENDENT   A self-contained claim setting forth all of its elements and limitations, none being included by reference to another claim. See *claim, dependent; fees; in extenso*.

CLASSIFICATION   Of patents, an elaborate system in the Patent andTrademark Office of official numbered classes and subclasses defined by subject structure and/or function, into which all patents and applications are fitted. Governs both the assignment of applications to examining groups and the organization of patents for search purposes. The system is set out in the official *Manual of Classification*. See *Manual*. Each Examiner works full time in a certain set of classes or subclasses of *art*. The search files in the Public Search Room and in the Examining Groups follow the same classification. Any search typically covers several subclasses of related art, unless a 'pat' *reference* is found right away, which is uncommon if the inventor knows his subject. The work of classification is difficult because, by definition, every patent is different from every other one. See *function, search, examiner*. There is also an International classification, which is different.

CLASSIFICATION DIVISION   In the Office, a special group responsible for maintaining the classification system and keeping it up to date, and for settling disputes between Examining Groups as to which one gets a given application. Staffed by experienced Examiners.

CLOSED   Of the *prosecution* of an application, the stage where no further *amendment* touching the *merits* is permitted — not including *final rejections*. Usually, the stage when all claims remaining in the case are allowed. Such an *action* cites the decision *Ex Parte Quayle*, 1935 *C.D.* 11. The applicant may want to submit additional, broader claims after such an action. He can't.

CLOSURE (mechanics)   Anything used to close or cover an opening, e.g., a cork, cap, cover, lid, plug. Commonly used in patent practice, for precision and breadth.

CODE OF FEDERAL REGULATIONS (CFR)   A costly shelf of government paperbacks. One volume, Title 37, contains copies of what were once all the rules of practice in patent and trademark cases, but with a more complicated numbering system. Rule 84, e.g., "Standards for Drawings", has become 37 CFR 1.84. Revised annually and sold by the Government Printing Office. The 1968 edition of the Rules sold for 55 cents. The 1977 edition of 37 CFR sold for $3 but had the added feature of poorer typography. See *Rule*.

COMBINATION   A group or assembly of parts or *elements*, or a series of steps in a process, which *define invention* because they coact or cooperate in some *unobvious* way to produce a *new result*. The term *combination*, if *new*, implies patentability. If, however, there is no new or unobvious coaction or cooperation between the elements, but each operates simply in its usual way, it is not a combination but an *aggregation*, and as such, not patentable. A court once adjudged a pencil with an eraser on the end an *aggregation*, and the patent on it *invalid for lack of invention*. (There is some new cooperation: the pencil is a handle for the eraser.) See *Old Combination, aggregation*.

COMMISIONER OF PATENTS AND TRADEMARKS   Chief executive of the Patent and Trademark Office. Presidential appointee, to date always a qualified patent attorney. His

superior is the Secretary of Commerce. The correct addressee for all communications to the O
fice is:

Commissioner of Patents and Trademarks
Washington, D.C. 20231

The correct payee for all checks is: 'Commissioner of Patents and Trademarks.'

COMPLICATED PROSECUTION (colloq.) *Prosecution* of an *application* through the more
unusual, complex, and time-consuming kinds of proceedings in the Patent Office, such as *interferences, appeals, continuations, reissues.* Interferences are the most complicated. The world's
record for complication is said to be held by one of the Gubelmann calculating machine
applications which was filed in 1912, went through 123 interferences over a period of 19 years,
and issued as patent No. 1,817,451 in 1931. (Gubelmann, a man of talent, won all the interferences and retired wealthy). The *file wrapper* of this case is said to occupy three feet of shelf
space. It has been estimated, however, that less than 2 percent of all applications become involved in any substantial complications, and only about 0.6 percent in interferences.

COMPRISING A prefatory term generally used in *claims.*
Ex.:
1. A process for making synthetic diamonds, *comprising* the following steps:
    (a) . . .
    (b) . . .
    (c) . . ., etc.

More definite than "including" but broader than "consisting of," which latter is not used because
it implies the exclusion of additional *elements.*

CONFLICT Not a recognized procedural term in the U.S. See *interference.*

CONTINUATION A copy of a pending application, filed in its place with a new filing fee and
new claims. The effect is to start the proceedings all over again. Useful in special circumstances.
Has benefit of filing date of *parent* application. Normally, the same Examiner will get it. He is
permitted, if it is apppropriate, to make a *final rejection* on the first *action.*

CONTINUATION-IN-PART (abbr. CIP) An application containing some matter the same as
in a prior pending application of the same inventor or ownership, plus some additional disclosure. Gets the benefit of the filing date of the parent case for only the matter shown in it; and
its own filing date for the remainder. Used in special circumstances, e.g., where the invention
described in the parent case turns out to be poorly-workable and a good improvement is invented later. The applicant is not required to point out which matter in the *CIP* is common to the
earlier application and which is newly added. Sometimes there are chains of CIP's, as the inventor invents improvements.

CONVENTION, INTERNATIONAL Agreement between all major industrial countries
relating to rights of their nationals to obtain patents in all the countries, and to obtain the benefit
of foreign filing dates in patent applications. An applicant filing in one country may obtain the
benefit of that filing date in another country if he files there within one year, the filing date of the
later foreign application being in effect the same as that of the first. The detailed provisions are
complicated. The Convention goes back to the 1880's, and contains other provisions relating to
trademarks and copyrights. Administered by the World Intellectual Property Organization
(WIPO) located in Geneva, Switzerland. See *priority, European Patent, Patent Cooperation Treaty*

COPY, CERTIFIED Xerox or other machine copy of a patent application or other pertinent
document, prepared by the Patent and Trademark Office and ribboned with a signed certificate
stating that it is a true copy. Bought from the PTO. Of applications as filed, needed to claim
Convention priority when filing some foreign applications.

COPY, HARD (colloq.) In the Office, a copy of a patent printed on special stiff durable paper
for use in the search files. Stapled at the bottom. Occasionally, one may turn up in an outside
order for *soft copies* (see below).

COPY, SOFT (colloq.)   Ordinary copy of a patent as sold by the Patent Office to the public, on ordinary paper. Currently, some are printed and some are less-legible machine copies from reels of film in a big machine built by a contractor.

CORRECTION, CERTIFICATE OF   An official correction of typographical errors found in a patent after it is printed, and included in copies of the patent. Similar to an errata notice in a book. If an error is the applicant's fault, it costs him (currently) fifteen dollars; if it is a printer's error, it is free. Either way, it is the patentee's responsibility to find the errors and request the certificate.

COPYRIGHT   Not a direct concern of patent practice; however, another form of intellectual property, a legal property right in a creation of the mind, created by statute. Both patents and copyrights are authorized by the same clause in the U.S. Constitution. Patent lawyers often deal also with trademarks and copyrights. Copyrights are not granted by the Patent and Trademark Office but by the Register of Copyrights in the Library of Congress. Patents are expensive to get, copyrights cheap and easy. The reason may be that copyrightable material describes itself; you just submit copies of it. An invention has to be described and illustrated by someone, with particular attention to how it works and what is new about it. The work involved is often comparable to that of writing a magazine article.

COUNT   In an *interference,* a *claim,* usually, common to all the applications involved, and defining an issue of the interference. A complex and specialized matter.

DEFENSIVE PUBLICATION   Publication by the Office of the abstract of an application, on a specific request by the applicant which must include a waiver of patent rights and a *provisional abandonment* of the application. The file of the case is laid open to the public. The Defensive Publication is printed and included in the *classified search* files, and thus becomes available as a *reference* against any later applications. Defensive Publication practice is relatively complex and is not too often used. It is apparently employed when it appears to an applicant that the allowance of desirable claims is very unlikely but there is concern that some other party may later file an application on something similar and possibly, by some oversight, get a patent.

DESIGN   1. The subject of a *design patent:* "a new and ornamental design for an article of manufacture." See *patent.* 2. In the engineering sense, the term *design* implies a degree of obviousness or ordinary standard practice in the *prior art;* hence the word is avoided by applicants except in reference to the *prior art.* The term is sometimes used by *examiners* in the sense of implying obviousness; as, 'This feature of the alleged invention is considered a mere matter of *design.*' See *art, prior.*

DECLARATION   Substitute for an *oath,* not requiring notarization, and accepted by the Office in most situations where a sworn oath was formerly required, not including affadavits. A declaration includes a penalty clause for false statements. Usually used instead of an oath when filing an application. See *oath.*

DELAY   Undesirable property of some legal proceedings, cited, e.g., in *Hamlet,* Act III, Scene I. The Rules of Practice say that a practitioner's signature on an amendment or other document filed is accepted "as a representation that it is presented in good faith and not for the purpose of delay." The period between the filing of an application and the first Office action runs, very roughly, of the order of one year, and has changed little for over a century. Delay between the filing of an application and the issue of the patent may operate either for or against the business interests of the applicant. Not uncommonly, delay may work in his favor, as reflection will show. See *special, term.*

DEPOSIT ACCOUNT   A sum of money deposited with the Office and drawn against for paying various fees and charges, for convenience. Not currently usable to pay for copies of patents. Must be used at least once every six months, or be closed out. Minimum balance currently is $50. Generally used by attorneys and agents. Anybody may open one.

DESIGN AROUND   The legal and proper method of commercially using concepts in a patent without infringing it, by changing the design of the thing the patent shows so that the new design does not *read on* the patent's *claims*. *Narrow* claims are easier to design around than *broad* claims.

DIRECTED TO   Concerned with, relating to, about, intended for, designed for. Used in preference to such terms in respect to *disclosures, specifications,* and *claims*. Ex.: "Claim _____ is *directed to* the modification shown in Fig. _____ of the drawing."

DISCLAIMER   By a patent owner, a statement giving up certain claims in the patent or the right to certain coverage of certain claims. Done usually after a court of appeals holds the claims, or interpretations, *invalid*.

DISCLAIMER, TERMINAL   A means of avoiding a rejection on the ground of *double patenting* (very technical). Say you own a patent that is 3 years old which will expire in 14 years, and that you file an application that claims some matter that overlaps some claims in your patent—so that allowance of these new claims would have the effect of extending the coverage of this matter to $17 + 3 = 20$ years. Since anything over 17 years is illegal, the *terminal disclaimer* you file will say that you give up the claims in question as of the expiration date of the earlier patent, i.e., you agree that both patents will expire on the same date, one being 17 years old and the other 14.

DISCLOSE   To furnish information new to the matter at hand. The *specification* of an application or patent *discloses* an invention. The sum of the information is a *disclosure*. A more common term in legal and patent usage than in ordinary English.

DISCLOSURE DOCUMENT   A written description of an invention, or something thought to be an invention, sent to the Office with a fee for safekeeping for a limited time (currently, 2 years max.) for use as evidence if ever needed, e.g., in case of a patent application. The Patent Office acts merely as custodian of the document. The evidence is of: (1) the date the document was received, and (2) the fact that it was not altered or added to after that date. The Disclosure Document Program was started in 1968. A typical disclosure document may have perhaps 1 to 3 typed pages and 1 or 2 sheets of sketches or photos. It must be in permanent ink (a Xerox copy will do) on paper $8\frac{1}{2}$ in. by 13 in. or smaller. The following items are required:

1. One copy of the document.
2. Two copies of a one-page signed form saying in substance:

> Commissioner of Patents and Trademarks,
> Washington, D.C. 20231:
>
> The undersigned, being the inventor of the disclosed invention, requests that the enclosed document be accepted under the Disclosure Document Program, and preserved for two years.
>
> (name, address, signature)

3. One stamped return envelope, self-addressed.
4. Check for $10 payable to "Commissioner of Patents and Trademarks."

Mail all 4 items to: Commissioner of Patents and Trademarks, Washington, D.C. 20231. One of the item (2) forms will be returned in the stamped return envelope, with a date and serial number stamped on it. The Office undertakes to keep the document for 2 years, on the theory that that should be time enough to file a patent application. If an application is filed, it may be accompanied by a reference to the disclosure document, which will then be preserved longer. The Disclosure Document Program is not too heavily used; many authorities say that other forms of such evidence are as good, such as a description read and signed and dated by two witnesses who understand the invention. Nobody is absolutely sure.

DISPOSE (mechanics)   To locate or arrange some element or part or object in some specified working relation with another. Term widely used for breadth, particularly in claims. See *arrange*.

DISTINCT   Used in the strict sense of *different,* distinguished from something else. 35 U.S.C. 112: "The *specification* shall conclude with one or more claims particularly pointing out and *dis-*

tinctly claiming the subject matter which the applicant regards as his invention. . ." The claims, i.e., must distinguish between the invention and everything else. Also, the claims in a given application must be *patentably distinct* from each other. For an Examiner to require *restriction*, there must be claims directed to two or more *distinct* inventions.

DIVISION   Where an application contains claims on two or more different *(distinct)* inventions, the cancellation of the claims of one group and the filing of a second ("divisional") application containing that group, with a copy of the same specification; splitting an application into two or more applications. Also an application so split off (with another filing fee), a *divisional* application. An Examiner may *require division* or *restriction*, indicating in his *action* the groups of claims considered divisible. The applicant may comply with the requirement or may *traverse* it, giving reasons; if the latter, the Examiner can either *withdraw* the requirement or make it *final*. Compliance with the requirement consists in cancelling the claims in all but one of the groups indicated. The divisional application or applications can be filed at any time while the parent application is still pending, and get the benefit of its filing date.

Division is not uncommonly required, for example, where a case claims a process, an apparatus used in the process, and the product of the process. The hazard of a rejection on *double patenting* exists if an applicant divides voluntarily without being required to. This must be watched. The principle behind division practice is that there should be no more than one invention in a single patent. See *restriction, double patenting.*

DOCKET NUMBER   Number used by a patent attorney or agent to identify an application for his own records.

DOMINATE (law)   Of a *prior* patent, to have *claims* which cover, encompass, or include *(read on)* the invention of a later patent, so that the later patent could not be *worked* without *infringing* the prior patent. A patent on a basic material would *dominate* later patents on products made from that material. See *prior, work.*

DOUBLE PATENTING   A ground of *rejection* of *claims* in an *application* which cover the same subject matter as claims in a prior application by the same applicant, or owned by the same owner. The effect of *double patenting* would be to extend patent protection beyond the statutory 17-year term, which is illegal. A technically complex field. See *division, restriction, terminal disclaimer.*

DRAFTING   1. Of *claims*, writing them. 2. Of drawings, see *draftsman, patent.*

DRAFTSMAN, OFFICIAL   A drafting group *(branch)* in the Patent Office which passes on the acceptability of application drawings for technical quality, etc, and will also make corrections in drawings, where required, for a moderate charge. Empowered to declare a drawing, or part of it, *informal*, requiring correction or a new drawing. This opinion then appears in the Examiner's first *action* as an *objection*. The objection can be *overcome* by ordering the required corrections, etc. in a *Letter to the Official Draftsman*, which usually accompanies an *amendment*. A cost estimate can be obtained and a check sent, or the cost can be charged to a *deposit account*. Such corrections need not be made until a claim has been allowed. Costs for minor corrections have been running around $10-$20.

DRAFTSMAN, PATENT   A person competent to make technical ink drawings to Patent Office standards. A specialized branch of technical illustration, sometimes considered most nearly related to the preparation of illustrations for instruction books for complex equipment. A knowledge of perspective, shading, cutaway views, etc. is required. Some patent draftsmen are free-lance, some work in patent drafting firms, and some are employed full-time by patent law firms, corporations, or government agencies. Currently they charge around $60 per sheet. Patent drawings are *not* like engineering drawings.

DRAWING   The technical illustration that goes with an application. Must be in india ink on bristol board in a prescribed format. Must be supplied "if the nature of the invention admits". No-drawing cases are, in practice, a small minority, mostly chemical in nature. Drawings may make extensive use of block diagrams, flow charts, schematics, and cutaway views. The drawing should show only enough of the *prior art* to make the invention clear. It need not be to scale, nor show more detail than is needed to understand the invention. If an invention be, say, the mechanism of an instrument, it is unnecessary to show the cabinet. Drawings are best made by a professional *patent draftsman*. An apt amateur can, however, sometimes produce acceptable drawings after studying the Rules and inspecting some pertinent patents, particularly if the drawing is something simple such as a block diagram. Hand lettering is OK if reasonably good. An average simple application may have 1 or 2 sheets of drawing; a complex case may have many.

Drawings are not permitted to leave the Patent Office once filled, except to lithographic firms for the purpose of making copies for use in foreign or *continuing* applications. See *draftsman, paper*.

ELECTION   In an application containing a *generic claim* or claims, and claims directed to species under the genus, the Examiner may (and often does) *require election* of one of the species, provided he does not consider the generic claim or claims allowable. Whether or not the applicant *traverses* the requirement, he must *elect* one of the species for prosecution; the claims on the other species are held in abeyance pending a final determination of the allowability of the generic claim or claims. If a generic claim is allowed, claims to three species under that genus are permitted in one application. If a generic claim is not allowed, only one species can be claimed. See *division, restriction, traverse*. The practice tends to be complex.

ELEMENT   In a *claim*, one of the machine parts or things, items, process steps, etc. that make it up. If a claim be considered as being in the nature of a list, the elements would be the items in the list. The elements in the example below are asterisked:

Ex.:
In an internal combustion engine,
*a plurality of cylinders,
*a piston slideable in each said cylinder,
*a wrist pin in each said piston engaging
*a connecting rod, and
*a crankshaft . . .

EMBODIMENT   Any specific physical form which the concept or principle of an invention may take. In a specification, a detailed description of a *preferred embodiment* is required. Other embodiments may be described also. The description must include enough detail to enable one *skilled in the art* to make or practice it: usually more detail than is customary in descriptions of apparatus in scientific papers, but less than in shop drawings. The best guide is to read prior patents on the same subject. See *example, idea, skilled in the art*.

ENABLING   "Not 'enabling' " is a *ground of rejection* of claims as being based on a *specification* that is written in such vague or general terms as to fail to "enable a person skilled in the art to which the invention pertains to make and use the same" (Rule 71). There may be no way to fix the specification without adding *new matter* (which see), the only recourse then being to file a *continuation-in-part*. A chemical specification should always give detailed descriptions of some *examples;* this is also desirable in electronic cases. See *example*.

ENGAGE(mechanics)   Of mechanical elements or machine parts, to touch, push, or temporarily connect together in a manner to transmit, or to affect the transmission of, force or motion, e.g., as between gear teeth, between a pin and a hole, or between the key and the tumblers of a lock. Term widely used in *claims,* for *breadth*.

ENTER   By the Office, of an amendment submitted, to accept it officially and make it part of the case file. An amendment received after the expiration of the time period set, or not *responsive,* will not be *entered*. An amendment submitted after a *final rejection* may not be entered. A complex subject.

ESSENTIALLY   Popular engineering term, avoided in patent practice.

ESTOPPEL (law)   The barring of a party from taking some course of action because he has already done something else that is inconsistent with it. After cancelling a *broad claim,* for example, an applicant cannot interpret a remaining, narrower claim as having the same breadth (indirect estoppel). Formerly a common type of patent license agreement included a clause in which the licensee agreed not to attack the validity of the patent in court. By so agreeing, he was *estopped* (direct estoppel). This doctrine of *licensee estoppel* was overturned by the Supreme Court in the famous *Lear vs. Adkins* decision in 1969.

ETHICS "*Attorneys* and *agents* appearing before the Patent Office must conform to the standards of ethical and professional conduct set forth in the Code of Professional Responsibility of the American Bar Association . . ."(Rule 344). Among the things forbidden are breaches of confidentiality and the soliciting of business. *Registrants* are subject to disbarment for offenses.

EUROPEAN PATENT A patent that is good in any or all of the countries of the European Economic Community. Empowered by a treaty called the European Patent Convention. The new system became operational in mid-1978. It operates alongside the regular national patent systems and does not supersede them. A single application suffices, written in any of the three official languages, English, French, and German. The European Patent Office, being staffed by tri-lingual examiners, is located in Munich. Searchers are made in the International Patent Library at The Hague. It would seem that the new system would save the applicant money. However, it is rare for governments to voluntarily give up revenue. The fees are high. A patent attorney for a multinational corporation has estimated that the break-even point comes at about three European countries, i.e., that it is cheaper to file up to three separate applications in different countries of Europe in the usual way, but if four or more are wanted the European patent may be the best buy. The new system is just starting up at the time of writing and not fully operational. There are complicated legal problems involved in the choice, which are best left to an expert. One clear advantage of the European patent is that the applicant has eight months longer to decide what countries to file in, than he has under the old separate-country system. This advantage, along with the advantage of a standard format, is shared by applications filed under the Patent Cooperation Treaty (PCT), which see.

EXAMINER, ASSISTANT Office employee who reads *applications, amendments,* etc., makes searches of the *prior art,* decides what to do, and writes appropriate *actions.* The opposite number to the patent *attorney* or *agent.* Each Examiner is assigned more or less permanently to a particular group of *classes* or *subclasses* of *art,* and becomes well-informed, often expert, in that area of technology. There are about 1600 Examiners. Basic requirement for hiring is a B.S. degree in physical science or engineering. By tradition, an LL.B. degree has also been needed for promotion to *Primary Examiner* or higher. Many assistant examiners have attended law school at night. Many eventually resign and become patent attorneys or agents.

EXAMINER PRIMARY Chief of a *Group Art Unit* (formerly called a *Division)* of, typically, 5 to 10 Assistant Examiners. Responsible for all their official *actions.* Generally handles in person the more legally-complex cases. Colloq., *Primary.* The name at the bottom of an *action* is usually his.

EXAMINER-IN-CHIEF One of a number of very-high-level Office employees who make up Boards of Appeal. A panel of three hears each appeal.

EXAMINER, SUPERVISORY Formerly, a chief over a number of examining divisions assigned to related arts, e.g., all the electrical divisions. Now replaced by *Group Director.*

EXAMINER, LAW High-level Office employee empowered to act for the Commissioner in certain situations, e.g., signing patent grants, acting on *petitions to the Commissioner.*

EXAMINER OF INTERFERENCES High-level Office employee specializing in hearing *interferences,* working under a 6-man Board of Patent Interferences.

EXAMPLE In all *applications,* an "enabling" example or embodiment of the invention must be described in detail. Additionally, in chemical cases a number of *examples,* with specific ingredients, process steps, etc. should be given, enough to support the *scope* of the *claims.* In electronic circuit cases, at least one example is desirable in the form of a list of component values to fit the circuit diagram. In mechanical cases, the detailed description of the "preferred embodiment" is often sufficient; but other examples may be desirable to support the scope of the claims. Failure to give enough specific examples may draw a rejection of the claims as based on an inadequate disclosure, etc., a situation to be avoided. U.S. *Office* practice is more demanding in this respect than that of most foreign patent offices, particularly the German. See *continuation-in-part, new matter, enabling.*

EXAMINATION   In the patent system of a country, the whole process of *searching, rejection* or *allowance* of *claims, amendment, argument, reconsideration,* etc. that takes place between the *examiner* and the *applicant,* and upon which the issuance of a patent is predicated. It is this process that gives the patent a legal presumption of validity. See *Patent, Foreign.*

EXAMINATION, DELAYED   Examination of a patent application made at the applicant's request, some time after filing. Not part of U.S. practice, but done in Germany and Japan. In those and some other foreign countries, examination is not automatic but must be requested and paid for with an extra fee. The applicant may have up to 18 months to file the request. In Germany and certain other countries you can wait 7 years. A feature of *European* and *PCT* practice.

EX PARTE   Legal proceedings, such as the *prosecution* of a patent application, in which there is only one named party, the other party being, e.g., the Patent Office. Somewhat similar to *In re.* A decision of the Board of Appeals on an appeal by an applicant X, or a decision on a Petition to the Commissioner by applicant X, is headed *Ex parte X.* In the Judicial Branch of the Federal Government, i.e., Federal courts, all proceedings are *inter partes,* though one of the parties may be the People or the Commissioner of Patents. The Patent and Trademark Office is an agency of the Executive Branch. But *interferences* are *inter partes,* inside the *Office.*

EXPEDIENT   Term used in Office *actions* and in attorneys' and agents' amendments

EXPIRATION   Of a U.S. patent, 17 years after its date of issue. After expiration, a patent is no longer enforceable against infringers, but it does remain a part of the *prior art,* the same as any *published* matter. The *claims* of an expired patent are of no interest. Its *disclosure,* however, is always available to defeat any later attempt to patent the same thing, or to patent anything that is not *patentably distinct* from it. It is said that a safe way for a manufacturer to avoid possible infringement suits is to make a product exactly as it is shown in some expired patent. The *term* of a patent cannot be extended except by special act of Congress. See *publication.*

FEES   1. Money charged by the Patent Office for, e.g., filing or issuing an application, filing an appeal, etc. Currently, the base filing fee is $65, base issue fee $100, plus certain extra fees for claims and pages over specified numbers. From 1931 to 1965, the filing and issue fees were each $30. All Government fees are payable in advance. Checks are OK. 2. Money charged by patent attorneys and agents for preparing and prosecuting applications. Typically similar to those charged by general lawyers, e.g., $30-$60 per hour. Flat rates are often quoted for preparing and filing a complete application for patent; these are often cheaper, and may be of the order of several hundred dollars for a reasonably non-complex case. The fees should always be discussed and understood with the attorney or agent before any work is started. See *printing charge.*

FILE WRAPPER   The whole contents of the Patent and Trademark Office's file on an *application.* On one which has issued as a patent, it is called a *patented file,* and is available for inspection to anyone on request at the Public Search Room; or a copy of the file can be ordered at (currently) 30 cents per page. The files of *pending* applications are secret, and not ordinarily open to anyone except the applicant and his authorized representatives. There are exceptions, e.g., in interferences and NASA cases.

FILE WRAPPER ESTOPPEL   In the prosecution of an application, loss of the right to take some course of action (e.g., presenting certain kinds of claims) because of something previously done and on record in the file wrapper that is inconsistent with the proposed course. Occurs primarily in *appeals.* See *estoppel, secrecy.* Attorneys and agents maintain case files and normally furnish the inventor with copies of all documents; but the Office file is the official one.

FOREIGN PATENT   See *patent, patent cooperation treaty; patent European.*

139

FORM (law) Sample wording of a legal document, published somewhere for the purpose of being copied, followed, or paraphrased. Not necessarily a conventional printed form. **Ex.**: assignments; powers of attorney; notices of appeal. Over 50 forms are published in the *Rules of Practice*. There are books containing hundreds. The advantage of following a form is that it is considered a kind of insurance against leaving something out, or inadvertently running afoul of some unexpected technicality. Published forms are either official, as in the Rules of Practice, or follow a text that has been ruled OK by some court. Court-tested forms are not, it is said, necessarily written in the best possible way. If they had been, they would be less likely to have got into litigation. Patent practitioners generally use Xerox copies of the Office's petition and declaration form in new applications.

FORM, MATTER OF Anything in an *application* that fails to comply with some *statute* or *Rule*, but does not affect the *substance* enough to prevent giving the application a filing date and an *examination*. A repairable technical defect. **Ex.**: blurred lines or wrong kind of paper on drawing; wrong wording or missing date or signature on oath or declaration; allowed claim dependent on a rejected *claim*. The Examiner *objects* to matters of form. Correction may, usually, be delayed until a claim has been *allowed*. When an Office *action* rejects all the claims but requires compliance with a matter of form, it is often considered likely that there is something allowable in the case, if it is properly claimed.

FORMAL Relating to *matters of form*.

FRAUD ON THE PATENT OFFICE The obtaining of a patent through the use of fraudulent representations, e.g., false affadavits. In 1968 the Federal Trade Commission sued in a Federal court to declare void a patent on the drug tetracycline which was owned by Chas. Pfizer, Inc., on the ground that that firm had obtained the patent through false statements in an affadavit filed during the prosecution of the application, which concerned the operation of the process for making the drug. The FTC won. The Patent Office has no facilities for testing or checking technical facts in the laboratory, and so accepts affadavits on such matters at face value. Nor is the Patent Office empowered to act against a patentee for such fraud. Other Government agencies may be, such as the FTC. Allegations of such fraud are reportedly being used increasingly by defendants in infringement suits.

FUNCTION (pat. classification) What a machine, apparatus, or device does, in contrast to what it is structurally. The function of a drill press, e.g., is to drill holes; but its structure comprises a base, column, table, motor, spindle, quill, chuck, etc. Patents may be classified for search purposes either by structure or by function. Neither scheme is without flaws, since similar-appearing structures may perform quite different functions, and the same function may be performed by quite different structures. Official *classification* practice appears to be primarily by function, with cross-reference copies distributed liberally through those subclasses which show related structures. Many subclasses in the Public Search Room have more cross-reference patent copies than originals.

FUNCTIONAL A ground of rejection of *claims*. A *functional claim* describes a thing solely in terms of the result it gets, rather than in terms of what it is; it would thus cover every possible means of getting the result, without pointing out how. At present the actual *rejection* is made on the ground of indefiniteness, 35 U.S.C. 112. The principle being well-known, functional claims are said to be relatively rarely submitted in recent decades.

A "*means*" clause in a *claim* is *functional* in nature. In the 19th century, all such clauses were forbidden. Later, claims containing a number of such clauses representing a *combination* of *elements* (but never consisting of only one such clause) were upheld by courts, and claims containing such clauses are now specifically authorized in 35 U.S.C. 112, paragraph 3. "Means" clauses are very useful and widely employed. See *means*.

GENERALLY According to the manner indicated, but permitting reasonable variation from what was specifically written. A term used widely in *specifications* and *claims*, particularly in claims. **Ex.**: "A shaft *generally* tapered" means that it may be uniformly tapered from end to end, or tapered over only some part of its length, so long as the result elsewhere indicated is obtained.

GENERIC   Of a claim, one which encompasses two or more subsidiary forms of the invention (species) which may be specifically claimed in other claims. Ex.: The basic *claim* on Edison's phonograph, setting forth a stylus, diaphragm, moving record medium, etc., would be *generic* to both cylinder and disc machines. See *election, restriction.*

GEOMETRY   The vocabulary of plane and solid geometry is used wherever appropriate in specifications and claims; it is indispensable in describing in words the shapes of structures and the kinematics of machines. In mechanical cases, you can't do without it.

GOAL (colloq.)   In the Office, a work quota for Examiners. At present, measured in total number of new applications taken up plus number of final case dispositions (allowance or final rejection) per week. Formerly called a quota, and then measured in total number of official actions per week; a typical figure was 8 to 14. From unofficial reports and published statistics, an average *goal* appears to be about 3-4 per week, or a total of 16-20 hours of Examiner's time for the whole *prosecution* of an average case. The time required on individual cases and actions varies widely, since both the technical complexity and length of applications, and the complexity of the legal situations that they get into, are subject to great variation. Examiners do not always have an easy time.

GROUND OF REJECTION   Of a *claim*, one of the established reasons, under the statutes, Rules, and decisions, for rejecting it. There are many such grounds, all described in *MPEP*, which see for details. Currently, *actions* cite the pertinent section of the statutes under *35 U.S.C.* (see *Laws*) in rejecting claims. Rejection of a claim as defining something already shown in a cited *reference*, i.e., as *old* or lacking *novelty*, is made on 35 U.S.C. 102. If a claim defines something different from the showing in a *reference* (or in the combined showings of 2 or 3 references), but the Examiner takes the position that the difference would be *obvious* to one *skilled in the art* who had the references before him, he rejects it on 35 U.S.C. 103. If the Examiner takes the position that a claim fails to "particularly point out and *distinctly* claim" the invention, he rejects it as *vague and indefinite* and cites 35 U.S.C. 112.

In older practice, an Examiner might word a Sec. 102 rejection as, "Claim _____ is rejected as fully met by (reference)," or as "reading directly on (reference)." A Sec. 103 rejection might read, "Claim _____ is rejected as unpatentable over (reference), or "as obvious in view of (reference)," or as "lacking invention over (reference)," etc. Combination rejections under Sec. 103 might read, "Claim _____ is rejected as unpatentable (lacking invention, obvious in view of, etc.) over (reference A) in view of (reference B)." The principle is that if a person *skilled in the art* had in mind all the *prior art* that there is in the world, the invention as defined in the claim would still have to be unobvious. A hypothetical situation, as scholars have observed. A strongly-based Sec. 102 rejection (e.g., on a "pat" reference) tends to be fatal. Combination rejections under Sec. 103 imply a better chance of being overcome by *amendment.*

The usage in *Sec. 112* rejections (vague and indefinite) differs from art to art. A general style of claim acceptable in a mechanical subject may encounter a *vague and indefinite* rejection if used in electronic circuitry. Chemical practice is a specialty in itself. A good *specification* is important.

Some other grounds of rejection are: *Aggregation, Old Combination, Undue Multiplicity of Claims, Prolix.* Which see.

GROUP   1. In the Patent Office, a group of Assistant Examiners working under a Primary Examiner, more correctly called a *Group Art Unit.* Formerly called a *Division.* 2. A group of such units under a Group Director. Ex.: Group 280, under a Group Director, is titled *Physics;* Unit 281 under this Director is titled *Photography, Optics, Photocopying, Motion Pictures, and Illumination,* and is headed by a *Primary Examiner.* 3. In an *Office action* which requires *restriction* or *division,* a listed group of claims which are stated to define an invention *distinct* (separate) from those in other listed groups of claims.

HEREIN (law)   In this document, application, etc., and no other. Used for precision and brevity.

HEREINABOVE, HEREINBEFORE (law)   Above or earlier in this document, and nowhere else. Used for precision and brevity.

HEREINAFTER (law)   After this point in this document, and nowhere else. Used for brevity.

IDEA   A word avoided in patent practice. By statute, an idea alone is not patentable. The specification must describe an *embodiment* of the idea. Since both the idea and the embodiment take the form of descriptions on paper, the distinction may seem obscure. While the word *idea* is informally proscribed, *inventive concept* and *principle* are acceptable. The term *invention*, as regularly used in *specifications* and *amendments*, may come close to being a euphemism for *idea*.

IDENTIFICATION   Of an application, the data normally listed at the top of any amendment or other document filed, e.g.,

Inventor: JOHN DOE	Date: Feb. 33, 1971
Serial No. 123,456	Group: 112
Filed: Feb. 31, 1970	Examiner: R. Roe
For: PROCESS FOR MAKING	
SYNTHETIC EMERALDS	

Strictly speaking, the serial no. and filing date are sufficient for the Office to locate the case, but not convenient. See *Serial Number*.

IDIOMATIC   The kind of English in which applications are required to be written, i.e., the idiomatic English of the *art* concerned. If the invention is a loom, *heddle* is part of the language; if a lock, *dog, tumbler;* if it is a d.c. amplifier, *long-tailed pair, bootstrap, common-mode rejection.* The Examiner and everyone else who will read seriously the patent which hopefully ensues will know the pertinent language, except, perhaps, a Federal judge.

IMPROVEMENT PATENT   Very roughly, a French *patent of addition*, a German *petty patent,* etc. No counterpart in the U.S., where all patents are of the same legal type, whether their effect may be to found a large new industry or to save a penny in the cost of making a can opener. In a sense, every invention is an improvement on something else.

INCORPORATION BY REFERENCE   A reference to or mention of another patent in an application, having the effect of incorporating the whole text of the patent. Purpose is to save space and printing charges, usually in *divisional* and *continuation* cases. See *MPEP* for details. See *reference.*

INDEFINITE   An important *ground of rejection,* often used by examiners, usually combined with *vague,* on 35 U.S.C. 112.

INDUSTRIAL PROPERTY   English language edition of monthly international journal which publishes new laws relating to patents, trademarks, and copyrights; international treaties, worldwide patent statistics, etc. Subscription, 50 Swiss francs per year. Published by World Intellectual Property Organization *(WIPO)*, Geneva, which is supplanting the older *BIRPI.* Both are administrative organizations for international treaties on patents, etc., supported by the member countries, which includes about all the major industrial nations. It is not clear why the name is not "Intellectual Property."

IN EXTENSO   Manner or rewriting a *claim* in *independent* form, required by an *examiner* after rejecting a *parent claim* but allowing a *dependent claim.* Ex.: An action rejects parent claim 1 and states that dependent claim 2 would be considered allowable (i.e., would be allowed) if rewritten *in extenso,* i.e., rewritten to *set forth* all the *elements* in both claim 1 and claim 2. See *element, limitation, claim.*

INFERENCE, RECITATION BY   A fault in the language of a *claim* which draws a rejection as *vague and indefinite:* in general, the recitation of an element in, e.g., a subjunctive clause. Each element must be positively set down, like a list.

INFORMAL   Failing in some way to meet the *formal* requirements laid down for an application by a statute or Rule, e.g., a drawing in pencil or on the wrong kind of paper; an *oath* or *declaration* which lacks one or more of the required statements, or omits a signature or date. See *form, matter of; formal.*

INFRINGE   Of a *utility patent,* to make, use, or sell in the U.S. anything that *reads on* any of the claims of the patent. See *claim, read on. Method claims* can be infringed only by practicing the method or process. *Product* and *apparatus* claims can be infringed by making, using, or selling the product or apparatus in the U.S.

Of a *design patent,* infringement is based on copying or substantially duplicating the appearance of the thing patented.

Plant patent infringement requires the reproduction of the patented plant asexually, e.g., by cuttings rather than seeds (the plant patent law was intended, by Congressional policy, to exclude seed grains).

The remedy for infringement lies in suits in the Federal courts, and is outside the powers of the Patent Office. The statutes permit the recovery of treble damages, i.e., three times the profit made from the infringement. An infringement suit in the U.S. is said to be a complicated affair, requiring a great deal of time from expert witnesses, accountants, etc., and to cost the plaintiff upwards of $50,000. Less than one patent in every 300 ever gets into an infringement suit.

INFRINGEMENT SEARCH   Thorough and specialized search used by manufacturers planning new products. Object is to find any unexpired patents that might be infringed, concentrating on their *claims.*

INNOVATION   The process of developing an invention and putting it into production and public sale; introducing it into the economic system. A new commercial product, process, or service so introduced. Not a synonym for *invention,* and a term not used in patent practice.

INOPERATIVE   Incapable of working for the purpose intended. A *ground of rejection,* fairly uncommon, but invoked against perpetual-motion machine applications in the days when these were more popular. The statute does not say that an invention must work well to be patentable; it merely has to work some. One former Examiner reported that in four years on the job, he had occasion to write only one rejection on the ground of inoperativeness, and this was an extreme case where there appeared to be no possibility that the alleged invention, a medical device, could work at all for the purpose alleged. Many years afterward, the former applicant was indicted by a county grand jury for fraud.

INORGANIC FILLER (colloq.)   Verbiage put in a *claim* with the intention of giving the Examiner the impression that the claim is more *limited* than it really is, with the object of getting it allowed. Said to be readily recognized by experienced examiners.

INTELLECTUAL PROPERTY (law)   A property right in a creation or production of the mind, e.g., a patent or a copyright, or a recorded performance by an actor or musician. A patent has the legal attributes of personal property. Such rights are recognized by law in all countries. See WIPO.

INTERFERE   As a verb, avoided. The only form of the word in general use in patent practice is the specific noun *interference.*

INTERFERENCE   A proceeding held before the Board of Patent Interferences in the Patent and Trademark Office, a priority contest between two or more applicants whose applications claim common subject matter. The Office initiates interferences, notifying the parties concerned. In deciding the winner, both the dates of *conception* of the invention and the matter of *diligence* in *reducing the invention to practice* are considered. The first party to conceive the invention may lose an interference if he failed (diligently) to work steadily, toward filing an application or without large time gaps, at bringing it to a stage of development where it could be demonstrated. Interferences were set up, e.g., between telephone patent applications of A.G. Bell and Elisha Gray. An interference is said by some authorities to be the most complex legal proceeding in the world. Interference practice is peculiar to the U.S. In other countries, the patent is issued to the first party to file an application. A change to the foreign practice is sometimes advocated in the U.S. The arguments on both sides are complex. See *count, junior party, senior party.* The filing of an application is a *constructive reduction to practice* as of the filing date.

INTER PARTES   Any legal proceeding in which there are two named opposing parties, in accordance with the adversary system fundamental to common law: *Lear vs. Adkins; Sears*

Roebuck vs. Stiffel Co.; People vs. Manson. The plaintiff's name is written first. All court proceedings are *inter partes.* The Patent and Trademark Office is an agency of the Executive Branch of the Government, not the Judicial Branch, and so (except in interferences) its proceedings are *ex parte;* the applicant's opponent, not named, is the Office, if he can be properly said to have an opponent. An appeal by an applicant X to the Board of Appeals is titled *Ex parte X.* If, however, he appeals from there to the Court of Customs and Patent Appeals (part of the Judicial Branch), the case is retitled *X vs. Commissioner of Patents and Trademarks.* In court, the Commissioner will be represented by a lawyer from the Office of the Solicitor of the Office.

> "I have seen . . . a look of amazement on the face of a judge when he is first advised of the procedure by which patents are obtained. They are told that a patent monopoly is typically granted in a secret, *ex parte* proceeding . . ."
> —Abe Fortas (JPOS v. 53, p. 815)

INTERVIEW A face-to-face or telephone conference between an applicant or practicioner and an Examiner in charge of his application. Practiced in perhaps a large minority of cases. Requires the OK of the Examiner. Interviews are never permitted before the first *action* in a case, but the applicant always has a right to one interview after a *final rejection.* The details of usage are fairly complex. The principle is that all the business concerning the prosecution of an application must be in the written record, and that the primary method of transacting it is by correspondence. An interview should be arranged at least several days in advance. If an *associate* attorney appears for an interview, it will be expected that he has done his homework, and has full power to act. Any understanding reached as to, say, the *allowability* of *claims amended* in some certain way, must be confirmed in writing, and the written *amendment* must reflect accurately the oral understanding. In general, interviews are appropriate in the later stages of the *prosecution* of a case, and the applicant must come prepared with a definite proposal based on a clearly-understood issue. If you heard a tape recording of one, it might sound easy; but everyone is very alert.

INVENTION A patentable invention. First, it must be in the statutory class of patentable *subject matter.* In the case of an application for a *utility* patent, it must be for "a new and useful process, machine, manufacture (manufactured product), or composition of matter" (35 U.S.C. 101). Many important things, once new, fall outside the statutory category, such as discoveries in art, mathematics, psychology, economics, and business and finance. Methods of doing business are not patentable, nor are the rules of games. The patentability of computer programs has been before the courts. "Useful" implies some purpose considered socially beneficial; an invention in card-cheating equipment was adjudged not "useful" within the meaning of the statute.

Second, it must be novel, i.e., new. The test is that it must be absent from all publications, anywhere in the world. Publications are defined as anything printed or otherwise duplicated that is or was generally available to the public, such as books, magazines, journals, and patents. Private memos and letters do not count.

Third, an invention must be *unobvious* to a (hypothetical) person *skilled in the art* and aware of all the publications to which the invention pertains. The jet engine, for example, had to be unobvious to a conventional photographic chemist or physicist. The term "unobvious" (35 U.S.C. 103) implies a certain degree of inspiration or ingenuity beyond the regular requirements of the job. Authorities agree that there is no way to measure it, and that an invention viewed by hindsight tends to look much more obvious than it did at the time the invention was made. The statute takes note of this.

A newly-discovered law of nature is not patentable under the statutes, but a useful device based on the law may be. While Isaac Newton could not have patented his Second Law of Motion under present statutes, he could, if he wished, have patented the accelerometer.

See also *Plant patent, design patent, novelty.*

JPOS Journal of the Patent Office Society. Published monthly since 1917 by that society, an unofficial organization primarily of patent Examiners. Membership, about 900. Circulation, about

4,000. Publishes articles on patent law and related matters. Considered an important part of any good patent law library. Anyone may subscribe, at $7 per year.

JUNIOR PARTY   In an *interference,* the party who filed his application latest. See *senior party, interference.*

KNOWN   Described or shown anywhere in the *prior art,* or in public use, at any time in history prior to the filing of an application for patent. Often used in a specification to distinguish something that is not considered a part of the invention from something else that is. See *according to the invention,* its opposite. May be used, e.g., as follows: "The container 77 may be sealed in *known* manner;" "amplifier 31 may be of any suitable *known* type."

LACHES (law)   The loss of the right to do something because of waiting too long before asserting the right.

LAW, PATENT   The body of law relating to patents. It is based entirely on statutes enacted by Congress, and has no basis in common law — unlike, say the law of unfair competition. The U.S. statutes on patents are mainly in Title 35 of the U.S. Code (abbr. 35 U.S.C.), and take up about 41 pages. Based on these is the vast body of case law made of decisions of the Federal courts in patent cases. The statutes are based on the provision in Article I, Section 8 of the Constitution:
The Congress shall have the power to promote the progress of science and the useful arts, by securing for limited times to authors and inventors the exclusive right to their respective inventions and discoveries.

LAWYER, GENERAL (colloq.)   Any lawyer who is not a patent lawyer.

LAWYER, PATENT   A lawyer who is also registered to patent practice before the Patent and Trademark Office. See *registration.*

LEAD LINE   In a patent drawing, a line running from a *reference numeral* to the part or element that it designates.

LICENSE   An agreement between the owner of a patent (licensor) and another party (licensee) which permits the licensee to make, use, or sell the thing patented in return for (usually) royalty payments. Licensing is a complex and changing field requiring the services of a good patent lawyer experienced in license negotiations. The subject is outside the jurisdiction of the Office. Licenses are private contracts; disputes are hearable in State and Federal courts. They may also be of interest to the Anti-Trust Division of the U.S. Department of Justice. See *misuse.*

LICENSING EXECUTIVES SOCIETY   An organization primarily of business executives and corporate patent attorneys who work in the field of outside licensing of patents owned by the companies for which they work. Membership in 1970, about 3,000. Members have reported notable success in spreading the commercial use of new technologies by licensing.

LIKEWISE   In *specifications, similarly* is used instead.

LIMITATION   In a *claim,* any *element* recited, or other restrictive language such as the nature or field of use of the thing claimed. The more limitations, particularly the more *elements,* the more limited the *scope* of the claim. Ex.: A claim *reciting* elements A, B, C, and D would be infringed by anything having all four of them; it would not matter if it had more. But if it contained fewer elements, e.g., only A, B, and C, that thing would not infringe. The more limitations a claim has, the *narrower* and more *specific* it is; the narrower its *scope.* Attorneys and agents try to get the *broadest* claims allowed that they believe they are entitled to, i.e., those with the fewest limitations. In prosecuting an application, a claim containing elements A. . .D is said to be *limited over* a *reference* which shows only elements A and B, or B, C, and D, etc. — and hence not *anticipated* by that reference. See *anticipate, claim, element, reference.*

MAINTENANCE FEES (foreign patents)   In various foreign countries, including England, France, West Germany, Japan, and Switzerland, fees charged by their patent offices periodically during the term (life) of a patent, and required to keep the patent in force. Due usually at specified times, e.g., annually, or after 3, 5, 10 years after the date of issue. Not charged in the

INVENTORS GUIDEBOOK

OATH In an *application,* a notarized form in which the applicant swears that, among other things, he or she believes himself or herself to be the first, original, and true inventor, that the invention has not been in public use or on sale more than one year prior to the application, and that no foreign application on the same invention has been filed more than one year prior. One of the *formal* requirements. Required by statute. Rules 65-68. A *declaration* is permitted in place of the oath, and is usually used. The oath or declaration, the power of attorney, and the petition are usually combined on a one-page printed form, available from the Office, Xerox copies of which are regularly used by attorneys.

OBFUSCATION As a word, not used. As a tactic, against the rules.

OBVIOUS The key word, together with its negative *unobvious* in determining whether an alleged invention is in fact a patentable invention in view of the *prior art.* 35 U.S.C. 103 (a key section in the patent statutes): "A patent may not be obtained though the invention is not identically disclosed (in the prior art) if the differences. . . are such that the subject matter as a whole would have been *obvious.* . . .to a person having ordinary skill in the art to which (it) pertains . . ." You cannot go to your local college placement bureau. hire an ordinary run-of-the-mill drawing-board engineer, instruct him to design an improvement in some product, and expect the result to be patentable — unless the hiree has thought up something above and beyond the call of duty. In Office *actions,* claims are often rejected as "obvious in view of *(reference* or *references),"* citing 35 U.S.C. 103. See *art, invention, skilled in the art.*

OFFICE When capitalized, the Patent Office. Its official full name was changed in 1975 to *Patent and Trademark Office,* but the old short name is still used.

OLD Not new; not *novel;* shown in a *reference.* An *action* may say, e.g., "Applicant's structure is *old* in the Jones reference," or, "Jones shows it to be *old."*

OLD COMBINATION A technical *ground of rejection* of claims, for including elements of a larger combination which itself is not a part of the invention. Ex.: a claim on the combination of a gasoline engine and an improved carburetor, where the alleged novelty is all in the carburetor and there is nothing new in the relationship between the carburetor and the engine. The claim should be on the carburetor itself. Relatively rare. See *combination.*

OPERATIVE RELATION Broad, self-explanatory term sometimes used in *claims,* e.g., "a cam in operative relation to a valve."

OPINION A court may write an *opinion* which discusses the reasons for its decision, but it doesn't have to. Examiners don't write opinions, only *actions* (or *Office letters*), but these must include reasons for their *decisions* (if an action is *final*) or their *positions* (if not final). When a case is appealed to the Board of Appeals, the examiner has to write an *Examiner's Answer.*

OR In claims, forbidden as *alternative language.*

OR THE LIKE Phrase sometimes permissible in the title of an application, often used in *specifications,* and sometimes in the introductory clause of a *claim;* but not in the main body of a claim.
> A trap for rodents or the like, comprising:
> a bait carrier,
> a wire bail,
> a spring . . .

PAPER A material subject to certain *formal* requirements. U.S. applications must be typed on 8½" by 13" or 14" paper in "permanent ink." "Easy-erase" typing paper is not acceptable; if an application is submitted on this, the Office will charge the applicant for making permanent copies for its own use. Currently, these are Xerox copies. A Xerox is permissible for the original copy of an application or other document as filed, and is often what is actually supplied. The copy supplied must be machine-reproducible. It should be noted that few jobs require as much reading as an Examiner's, much of it in poor light. The applicant may consider this from humanitarian motives.

146

ticing (operating) the method claimed in the U.S. An apparatus or product claim can, however, be infringed by either making, using, or selling the thing claimed in the U.S. A product patented in the U.S. cannot be sold without permission in this country even though manufactured abroad. The product of a process claimed in a U.S. patent can, however, sometimes be sold in the U.S. without infringement of the U.S. patent if the claimed process is practiced abroad. This last point is currently under debate. The distinction between method claims and apparatus or product claims often occurs in questions of *restriction* or *division,* which see.

METRIC SYSTEM   The use of the metric system for measurements is at present "strongly encouraged but not mandatory" in patent applications. Measurements may be all in metric or in English units with the metric equivalents in parentheses.

MISUSE, PATENT (law)   Illegal use of a patent for the purpose of gain. **Ex.:** A license to make or use patented card-punch machines which required the licensee to buy unpatented cards from the licensor ("tying"). A matter for the Federal courts, outside the powers of the Office. A complex and changing field, in recent years of interest to the Anti-Trust Division of the Department of Justice.

MONOPOLY (patent law and general law)   Term not used in Patent Office practice, but a subject of controversy in patent law journals. By one view, a patent is a 17-year monopoly, and so shares the anti-social characteristics of all monopolies, such as a monopoly on medicine or milk. By the other view, the subject of a patent never existed before, and hence is no more a monopoly than the copyright on a book. All governmental agencies and some businesses are monopolies.

MPEP   Manual of Patent Examining Procedure. Official book prepared by a staff group in the Office and followed by Examiners. Prescribes procedures under the statutes and the Rules of Practice for coping with virtually every procedural situation that may arise in the prosecution of an application. Attorneys and agents are presumed to have copies. A big loose-leaf book about 2 inches thick, extensively revised at frequent intervals. Sold on a subscription basis by the Superintendent of Documents, Government Printing Office.

MULTIPLICITY   A ground of rejection of claims, used by Examiners when the number of claims in an application appears to be far larger than actually needed. Fifty claims, for example, might be appropriate on an application for a very complicated machine; but fifty claims appended to a relatively simple *specification* of, say 6 pages, might well draw a rejection as *unduly multiplied.* In current practice, the *assistant Examiner* would make a phone call to the applicant, asking him to select no more than a specified number of claims for examination, and would then include a rejection of all the claims as *unduly multiplied* in his *action.* Not a common situation.

NEGATIVE LIMITATION   In a *claim,* language *reciting* the absence of something, e.g., "a shaft without a flange," or "a white pigment without lead compounds." Not generally permitted. *MPEP* gives certain borderline exceptions. In general, a claim containing a negative limitation will be rejected as *indefinite.* There are exceptions.

NEW MATTER   Information, data, descriptive matter, or any *disclosure* which goes significantly beyond what was in the *specification* as originally *filed.* The addition of *new matter by amendment* is not permitted. The Examiner is empowered to refuse to enter an amendment which he rules to contain *new matter.* The reason is that the original filing date of the case is good only for what was received on that date. An invention *B,* disclosed in an amendment filed in August, may not become part of an application that disclosed only an earlier invention A, filed the preceding March. If an inventor thinks up important improvements after an application has been filed, they should go either in a separate application or in a *continuation-in-part.* Ordinary corrections of obvious errors and simple clarifications of minor points do not generally constitute new matter, and are usually OK. It is important to get all the important points in the application as filed, so far as possible.

NO GREATER THAN   A phrase permissible in, and often used in, claims, as having that specific meaning. The popular expressions *up to,* and *as much as* are, however, considered *indefinite* and not used.

147

U.S. Sometimes advocated in the U.S. as a way of charging the owners of patents which are *worked* and bring in a profit, in contrast to the majority of patents which are not. An argument on the other side is that an invention patented ahead of its time (as many have been) may be incapable of paying off until late in its term — by which time the owner may well have given up paying maintenance fees and have nothing left.

MARKUSH GROUP (chem. patent claims)   In a *claim*, a kind of artificial group of elements permitted only in chemical cases. If, for example, an inventor finds that either chlorine, bromine, iodine, or sulfur will work in a certain reaction, but not fluorine, he cannot claim a "halogen;" but under the Markush practice he can write a claim with language such as:

" . . .any one of the group chlorine, bromine, iodine, or sulfur . . "

The authority for the practice is a Commissioner's decision over 40 years ago, in *ex parte Markush*, 1925 C.D. 126.

Such artificial groups are not permitted in non-chemical claims. If, say, there is a need in a mechanical case to put into a claim as a broad element, "belts or chains but not gears," it can't be done, because *or* is an *alternative expression,* and *not* introduces a *negative limitation,* both forbidden. The claim draftsman has to find some other way to say it, such as "endless flexible mechanical driving means." A specialized matter. matter.

MANUAL OF CLASSIFICATION   Published list of all the official Patent and Trademark Office classes and subclasses of patents, for search purposes. Assignment of applications to Examining Groups is based on the Manual. It is a thick loose-leaf book, prepared and frequently revised by the Office. Copies are for sale by the Superintendent of Documents, Government Printing Office, on a subscription basis. Cost, around $50 per year. Copies are available in the larger public libraries. It is the basic reference for making a *pre-ex* or other search.

MATHEMATICS   Has no special meaning in patent pratice, but its use requires comment. It is permissible in *specifications* and *claims* wherever it offers the best language in which to explain the invention. Should not be used for the primary purpose of impressing the beholder, as is sometimes the practice in engineering and scientific journals and in reports by corporate and government researchers.

MAY   1. Can; is permitted to but not restricted to. A more definite term than *can* or *could,* but much less restrictive than *must.* In patent applications, used to introduce examples without implying restriction to those examples. Ex.: "The carburetor float may be made of sheet brass . . ." connotes that sheet brass is a good material for the purpose, and possibly the best; but it does not exclude any other material that will serve the purpose. 2. (law) Has the power or authority to do something, with no implication as to how likely he is to do it. Ex.: "The Commissioner may grant a petition to . . ." (or may not).

MEANS   Any apparatus or device or machine part or process step that will produce a stated result. Term used widely in *claims,* e.g., "means for rotating," "synchronizing means," "cooling means." The last would cover, e.g., a mechanical refrigerator, an ice bag, or a thermoelectric cooler, all without using any of the forbidden *alternative language* such as the word *or.* The "means" clause in patent claims is itself an invention, at first struck down by the courts a century ago, then later upheld and now established practice. A single "means" clause may not, however, constitute a whole claim. See *functional.*

MERIT, MERITORIUS   1. (law) Of a party's argument or position, its soundness. Ex.: "Appellant's argument is without merit," i.e., full of logical holes, or based on a poorly-proven set of facts. 2. Quality of usefulness or effectiveness, as a "meritorius invention." 3. MERITS In an application, the significant content of the *claims* that concerns their patentability over the *prior art,* as compared to *matters of form.* See *action, closed, formal.*

MESNE (law)   Of *assignments,* intermediate. On a patent, the heading, "X, assignor, by mesne assignments, to Z" means that X first assigned it to some other party Y, who in turn assigned it to Z. Or there may have been other intermediate assignees Y1, Y2, . . .(pron. "mean").

METHOD CLAIM   A *claim directed to* a method or process, in contrast to a claim for an apparatus. machine, or product. A method claim in a U.S. patent can be infringed only by prac-

Drawings must be in india ink on 8½" by 14" bristol board; there are detailed requirements set out at length in Rule 84. The reason for india ink is reproducibility for printing the patent. The reason for bristol board is erasability. Minor corrections are fairly often required. Legal paper is long because it's fastened together at the top.

PARENT APPLICATION A prior application of the same applicant which has the same specification as (or contains matter common to) a later application which depends on it, and is filed while the parent application is still pending. The later application is usually a *division* or a *continuation* or a *continuation-in-part,* and must contain a reference to the parent application. There are also such things as grandparent applications, etc.

PATENT A grant by a government of the right to exclude others from making, using, or selling an invention as claimed in a patent document, for a period (in the U.S.) of 17 years from the date of its issue. By statute, a patent has the legal attributes of personal property. As such, it does not convey the right to make, use, sell, etc., but only the right to exclude others. See *dominate.*

In theory, a patent has been considered a contract between the inventor (or owner) and the public. The inventor gives to the public the *disclosure,* i.e., makes public the previously-secret and presumably-valuable knowledge in it; and the public (the Government) gives the inventor in return the 17-year exclusive right. The inventor's contribution is written and illustrated in the *specification.* The boundaries of the Government's grant of 17-year exclusivity are defined in the *claims.* The claims define what can and cannot be infringed. Hence the claims are the central issue in the proceedings before the Examiner in the Patent Office, and also in court litigation of patents.

The sole authority to grant U.S. patents is in the Commissioner of Patents and Trademarks. But a Federal court can hold some or all of the claims of a patent *invalid,* and often does. See *valid.*

PATENT COOPERATION TREATY (PCT) An international treaty which, among other things, authorizes the national patent offices in the member countries to accept the results of searches made in designated offices of other countries (including the U.S., England, West Germany, The Netherlands), and prescribes a standard international format and three official languages for applications, English, French, and German. The treaty became operational in mid-1978 and includes the U.S. and all the industrial countries except Japan. Japan is said to be expected to sign shortly. There are numerous other provisions in the 55-page treaty; a short summary is impossible. The U.S. Patent Office is one of those designated a Receiving Office. It will accept an application in PCT format when accompanied by the required fees and forms designating the other countries in which the applicant desires filing. The format requires "A4" size paper for both text and drawings, 29.7 by 21 cm or about 11¾ by 8¼ inches. The typing must be 1½ spaced. Organization and page numbering have special requirements. A prominent attorney has estimated that during the first few years of PCT operation only a minor percentage of applications will go the PCT route. In accordance with the principle that no government gives up revenue or gets along with fewer civil servants, the PCT fees are high, cancelling out the apparent saving from simplification. One authority says that initially it will effect cost savings only where more than about three foreign filings are to be made. In the long run it will be advantageous. One clear advantage of PCT filing, like the European Patent, is that the applicant has eight months longer to decide what countries to file in after he has filed in the first. See *Patent, Foreign, European Patent.*

PATENT, DESIGN A patent on the appearance of a utilitarian object, required to be "ornamental," as contrasted to a *utility patent.* Design patents are separately numbered, and currently form about 7 percent of the total, or around 250,000. Design case practice is simplified, fees are lower, and only one claim, formal in nature (i.e., stereotyped) is permitted. Design patents are often used by manufacturers of "styled" products and concern only the product's appearance. Car bodies, furniture, lamps, bottles, toys, ash trays, glassware, type faces, rugs, store fronts and buildings (such as chain hamburger stands) are popular subjects. By statute and rules, the *ornamental design* patented must *involve invention.* Some scholars think that this kind of *invention* is hard to define, and that a design patent, although granted by the Patent Office, is more in the nature of a copyright. The copyright statutes do not, however, provide for copyrighting the appearance of any manufactured product which also has some other kind of utility. All design applications are examined in the Design Group of the Office.

PATENT, FOREIGN Over 100 countries have patent systems. The Republic of Texas and the Confederate States of America had them. A patent is good only in its own country; e.g., a product patented in the U.S. but not in France could be freely made, used, or sold in France; but importation and use or sale in the U.S. would infringe. The *international convention* gives certain rights of application and priority (of filing date) to residents of all member countries. Currently, an estimated 30-42 percent of all U.S. patent applications come from applicants residing abroad. To obtain a patent in a foreign country it is necessary to employ a patent agent registered in that country. Some U.S. practitioners deal directly with foreign agents; others use one of several U.S. firms which specialize in foreign practice, some having branch offices abroad. Very roughly, the patent laws are somewhat similar in the major industrial countries, e.g., England, Japan, West Germany, The Netherlands, the Scandinavian countries, Czechoslovakia, Switzerland, and the U.S. To the specialist, however, the differences appear great. Translations pose problems. A translator, however fluent in the languages concerned, cannot make a good translation of, say, a chemical patent unless he also has a knowledge of chemistry. Every country requires patent applications to be written in its own language.

Russia has a patent system and is a member of the *international convention*. It is reported, however, that Russian nationals are discouraged from applying for patents, being encouraged instead to apply for *author's certificates*. These are reportedly in the nature of suggestion box entries, and qualify for awards of money at that government's discretion. Most Russian patents are owned by foreigners.

The patent offices in only the more heavily industrialized countries have *examination* systems, e.g., U.S.A., England, West Germany, Canada, Australia, Russia, the Netherlands, and the Scandanavian countries. Other countries, notably Italy, Spain, and in Latin America, use the much simpler *registration system*. Under this, there is no examination nor search for novelty, but the application is simply registered for a fee. Usually there are no *claims*. The questions of novelty, inventiveness, etc. are left to the courts, if and when a patent gets into litigation.

Before mid-1978 all foreign patents (with a few exceptions) were obtained separately in each individual country in which a patent was desired, using a foreign agent registered in each country. Now there are two other routes, both new and operating in parallel with the regular individual foreign patent systems and procedures.

A *European patent* is good, as of early 1978, in Belgium, West Germany, France, Holland, Switzerland, and England. Italy, Norway, and Sweden are expected to ratify the European Patent Convention in 1978. There is a European Patent Office in Munich, with a branch at The Hague where the searches are made (in the International Patent Library). The governing Convention is related to the activities of the EEC. The system is not fully operational as of late 1978 and is not expected to be for a few years. The fees are high. It is said that it is more expensive than about three separate patents in European countries obtained in the old-fashioned way, and so is at present of interest mainly to industrial firms who seek patent protection in several countries.

The *Patent Cooperation Treaty* (PCT) includes the U.S.A. and all the main industrial countries except Japan. It offers a simplified procedure for applying for patents in several countries, with a standard format, uniform rules, and a choice of three official languages (English, French, and German) like the European patent, to reduce translation costs. Like the European patent system, the PCT is just starting up and operates as a minor adjunct to the regular national systems; its fees are high and considered by some attorneys to be not worthwhile at present unless more than about three foreign patents are to be applied for.

Both the European patent and the PCT route offer advantages in time. It is possible to wait several months longer after the initial filing to designate the countries desired, than is possible with the regular separate-nation system. The procedure in both are complex, new, and untried, and appear to be viewed with caution by many attorneys, who at present may prefer to call in a firm that specializes in foreign practice in order to avoid unforeseen pitfalls.

See *Convention, European Patent, Patent Cooperation Treaty.*

PATENT, IMPROVEMENT See *Improvement patent.*

PATENT PENDING A notice marked on a manufactured article that a patent is pending, i.e., has been applied for and that the application has neither been abandoned nor issued as a patent. Serves as a warning that a patent may issue at some future date. Infringers cannot be sued until a patent has actually been issued. A patent pending *(syn. patent applied for)* notice is optional, not compulsory; but a false notice is illegal.

PATENT, PLANT Patent on a new variety of plant. The plant must be capable of asexual reproduction, e.g., from cuttings rather than seeds. Novelty is determined by the U.S. Department of Agriculture, the Patent Office acting as intermediary. New varieties of roses are often patented. Plant patents were first authorized in 1930. Total number to date, about 1000. The illustrations on plant patents are usually reproductions of color photographs. Practice in the prosecution of plant patent applications is in a general way similar to that in *design* cases.

PATENTED FILE The whole contents of the Patent Office file of an application that has become a patent. Open to the public for inspection on request at the Public Search Room. May be voluminous. A copy may be ordered. Current charge is 30 cents per page. Patented files are perused by attorneys acting for potential buyers, licensees, and infringers. See *secrecy.*

PARENTHESES To be used with caution in patent practice to the same extent as in ordinary technical English. Not permitted in *claims.*

PATENT OFFICE Name changed to Patent and Trademark Office in 1975. Old name is still used. Agency of the U.S. Department of Commerce having sole authority to grant patents and register trade marks. Chief executive is the *Commissioner of Patents.* Has about 2600 employees, of which about 1600 are Examiners. Maintains a Public Search Room, a good scientific library, a stock of printed (or on film) copies of all U.S. patents for sale; registers attorneys and agents to practice before it; various other services. Formerly located in the Commerce Department Building ("Hoover's Folly"), 14th & E Sts. NW, Washington, D.C., erected 1928. Now in leased quarters at Crystal Plaza, Arlington, Va. Correct mail address is, however, "Commissioner Of Patents and Trademarks, Washington, D.C. 20231."

The Office receives roughly around 100,000 applications per year, and issues around 60,000 patents. These very approximate figures have not changed in any major way in over 50 years. The Office is an agency of the Executive Branch of the Government. As such, it has no power in matters such as infringement and licensing, this being reserved by the Constitution to the Judicial Branch, i.e., the Federal courts. See *ex parte, Commissioner of Patents, Examiner.*

PATENT, UTILITY A patent on a machine, article of manufacture (manufactured product), process, or composition of matter (e.g., a chemical composition or mixture), directed to the technological nature of the invention. Also called a *mechanical patent.* About 92 percent of all U.S. patents are of this type. The rest are *design* patents or *plant patents,* which see. See also *invention.*

PENDING Of an *application,* filed but neither abandoned nor issued as a patent; still having the status of a live application.

PERIOD FOR RESPONSE A time period ending in a deadline for *response* to an Office *action* or letter. Given at the beginning of the action. The maximum period for response is set by statute at six months, but may be and usually is set under the Rules at a shorter time by the Examiner. Most often it is set at three months from the date the action is mailed. Where the *response* required is only a *matter of form,* the period is often set at one month. One request for a 30-day extension may be expected to be granted if reasonably good reasons are given in a written request. The request must be made within the period originally set, preferably well within the period. If no *response* is received at the Office within the period set, the case is held *abandoned* (for lack of prosecution). See *abandon.* The period for response is to be taken seriously. There are similar deadlines for payment of issue fees, etc.

PETITION 1. In a patent application, a brief formal statement saying that the applicant is asking for the grant of a patent. Usually part of the combined petition, declaration (or oath), and power of attorney form stapled to the application. 2. *Petition to the Commissioner.* Procedure used by applicants who disagree with a decision of an Examiner on matters that are not appealable, i.e., do not relate to the *merits.* Petitions may be taken, e.g., from a final requirement for *restriction,* from non-entry of an *amendment,* from a holding of *abandonment.* A petition may be filed to make an application *special.* Most petitions carry no fee; there are exceptions. Statistically, a petition to the Commissioner is filed in roughly 1 out of every 7 or 8 applications filed, on one issue or another. Usually, such petitions are taken up by a *Law Examiner.* Rule 183, while very rarely invoked, is of interest:

> In an extraordinary situation, when justice requires, any requirement of these Rules which is not a requirement of the statutes may be suspended or waived by the Commissioner in person on petition of the interested party, subject to such other requirements as may be imposed.

Some petitions require supporting affidavits. See *special.*

PICTURE CLAIM (colloq.) A claim which is so detailed as to describe a detailed "picture" of the embodiment of the invention claimed; hence, a claim so limited as to be readily *allowed* by the Examiner, but of relatively little value for use against infringers because it is easy to *avoid* by making minor changes in a product, etc. Said to have been often submitted by *advertising attorneys.*

PIECEMEAL Of the prosecution of an application, taking up part, instead of all, of the matters in issue, in either an *action* or *an amendment.* Piecemeal prosecution is not permitted either to Examiners or to applicants. A technical term.

PORTION A fraction or piece or percentage of something; a subassembly; everything significant in some general area of a device, as, the *upper portion* of a structure, the *skirt portion* of a piston. Widely used in claims for breadth and brevity. Used instead of the term *part,* which connotes a discrete object of some kind.

PERFECT The verb, as if to *perfect* an invention, is not used. The only term used in this general sense is to *reduce to practice,* which means to develop the concept of an invention to the stage of a demonstrable working model which proves that the invention works. See *interference.* The terms *develop* and *innovate* are not part of patent practice.

PRACTICE 1. The preparation and *prosecution* of *applications* for patents, and related matters, before the Patent and Trademark Office, for others for a fee. See *registration.* Generally similar in meaning to *practice* of law, of which it is a kind. 2. The whole body of statutes, rules, procedures, usages, etc. which govern the work of the Patent Office and of those who do business with it, e.g., attorneys, agents, and applicants. Sometimes called *Office practice.* 3. The actual physical operation of a working model of an invention. See *reduction to practice.*

PRACTITIONER, PATENT Any person *registered to patent practice* before the Patent and Trademark Office; a patent attorney or agent. See *Registration.* A member of the Patent Office bar.

PREDETERMINED Under the control of, determined by, or at the discretion of the designer, builder, inventor, or operator of a device, machine, or process — rather than being determined by some characteristic of the device or process itself. A term widely used in *claims.*

PRELIMINARY SEARCH A search of the *prior art* in the Office made by an inventor, attorney, agent, or professional searcher before an application is filed. May take 2 to 4 hours for a reasonably simple *disclosure.* A searcher may typically work from one or two pages of sketches and a page or so of description. If the *art,* i.e., the *references* found, is too close to the inventor's disclosure, it may be inadvisable to file an application. If the art is not as close as expected, it suggests that the application be written with *broader claims* than originally thought. Made in the *Public Search Room,* often with short excursions to the pertinent examining groups. Colloq., *preex.* See *Search Room.*

PRINTING CHARGE Government charge of (currently) $10 per page of printing of an issued patent, plus $2 per sheet of drawing, added onto the base issue fee of $100. One printed page in a patent equals approximately 4½ pages of Elite typewriter type on 8½" by 13" paper. The issue fee bill sent upon allowance of an application covers, at present, only the drawings and one page of printing. If the printed text comes out longer than one page (which it usually does), an additional bill is enclosed with the patent itself, on delivery. This *balance of issue fee* is due within three months, on pain of lapse of the patent. See *fees.*

PRIOR   Previous, earlier in time. Widely used because of its specific meaning. *Prior art* is e.g., patents or other published matter published before the filing date of the application in question. A *prior application* is, roughly, one that was *pending* before the filing date of another of the same ownership. *Convention priority* is the grant of an effective filing date on an application the same as the date of a corresponding foreign application filed earlier (but not more than 1 year prior). See *convention, statutory bar.*

PRIOR ART STATEMENT   A statement in a patent application, or filed later while it is *pending,* which lists the closest prior patents and publications the applicant knows of, and describes very briefly the pertinent points in them. "Permitted and encouraged" by the Patent Office since 1975. When included in an application it often is made part of the "Background" section of the *specification,* which is lately divided into two subsections, "Field of the Invention", and "Description of the Prior Art." A half-page or so is sufficient in perhaps the majority of cases.

PROLIX   A ground of *rejection* of *claims,* as being so unreasonably long or wordy as not to merit proper consideration. Not often encountered.

PROSECUTE   To handle all the business with the Patent and Trademark Office relating to an application, e.g., writing the application and amendments and other responses required; handling interferences and appeals. May be done by the inventor *pro se,* or by an attorney or agent appointed by him. The file of an application is the written record of its *prosecution.*

PROVIDE   To furnish, supply, or introduce as part of some device, system, process, etc. Generally used in preference to its synonyms. Ex.: "The microscope may be provided with a filar eyepiece..."; "A timing belt is provided to drive the camshaft."

PUBLIC USE   Use of an invention as by public display or commercial sale, in contrast to private or experimental use. Public use, public sale, or publication of an invention more than 1 year prior to filing a patent application constitutes a *statutory bar* to getting a patent. Treatises have been written on the subject of what the courts have held to be public use and what they have not. Private demonstration or private disclosure of an invention have been held not to be public use, and not a *bar.*

PUBLICATION   Anything printed or otherwise duplicated which is or was readable by and generally available to the public anywhere in the world at any time in history. Any *prior publication* is usable as a *reference* against claims in a patent application, for the purpose of *rejection.* Foreign patents, from those countries where they are published (all major industrial countries) count as publications. Authors Certificates, a suggestion-box-type institution of Soviet bloc (and a few other) countries, are now counted as publications.
   It might appear that old or exotic publications which might exist somewhere which would defeat some patents, were never found during the prosecution of their applications. Such occurrences are relatively rare, however, in real life. The case of the various patents on safety pins granted in the late 19th century furnishes a curious exception. Anticipatory safety pins had been made during the Bronze Age, c. 1500 B.C., but were still buried and unknown at the time. Years later, some were dug up and their photographs published in archaeological journals.
   The *Public Search Room* has U.S. patents only. The search files of the examining groups contain, in addition however, selected foreign patents and copies of pertinent magazine and journal articles. Examiners select and add material at their discretion, for their own files. Current technical periodicals are circulated to those groups whose fields of interest they fit, e.g., the *AMA Journal* to Group 335, whose field is Surgery and Prosthetics. The Office Scientific Library has an unusually complete collection of scientific and technical periodicals.

PURVIEW   Scope, field, limits or boundaries. Formerly a common term in patent *specifications,* as, "Many variations may be made within the *purview* of the invention." A term not often used nowadays.

153

READ ON Important technical term in patent practice, best defined by example. A claim *reads on* a *reference* if every *element* in the claim can be found in the reference. If fewer than all the claim elements can be found shown in the reference, the claim does not *read on* it. **Ex.**: The combination of a moving record with an undulating groove, a stylus engaging the groove, a diaphragm driven by the stylus, etc. would *read on* Edison's phonograph. But if a claim in a later case *set forth* these elements and in addition an electrical transducer connected to the stylus, an amplifier, and a speaker, it would not *read on* Edison. It would have something in addition, and, in its day, a patentable improvement.

RECEIPT 1. A filing receipt for a new patent application, form PO 103(a), printed on a slip of blue paper 3" by 5", mailed by the Office to the applicant or attorney or agent and giving the identification of the case, the filing date, and the Serial No. assigned and the Group to which it is assigned. Currently these have been one or two months late in arriving. Forms are also mailed acknowledging *Notices of Appeal.* Receipts are not sent for other documents, such as *amendments,* which custom, long ago, led to the following institution: 2. *Postcard Receipt.* For proof of delivery of amendments, etc., a stamped self-addressed postcard identifying the document and mailed with it to the Patent Office. There, the Mail Room applies a date stamp to it and drops it into the return mail. The postcard is universally used by applicants and practitioners.

RECITE Of *claims,* to say or state something. **Ex.**: "Claim 3 *recites* the temperature range of the process . . ." Syn. *set forth.* The word was formerly in more general use:
> Their walls are covered with inscriptions, and
> these *recite* the dates of their construction.
> —William H. Seward's *Travels Around the World,*
> 1873

REFERENCE 1. A specific *prior* patent or *publication cited* by an Examiner as being considered to show all or some part of the alleged invention claimed in a patent application. *References* are *cited against* claims, or *applied to* them in Office *actions.* The Examiner lists the *references relied on* on a form mailed with the *action.* Claims are also *rejected on* stated references. 2. *Reference to related application:* a statement in an application which identifies another application of the same inventor or owner, e.g., "This is a division of my copending application Serial No. _____, filed Feb. 30, 19____." In *divisions, continuations,* and *continuations-in-part,* such a reference to the *parent* application is required.

REGISTER As a procedural term, used in the U.S. only in respect to the *registration* of attorneys and agents and the registration of trade marks.

REFERENCE NUMERAL In a patent drawing, one of the numerals used to designate the parts of the thing illustrated. Letters are permissible instead of numerals, but are not often used. In U.S. patent *claims,* they are permitted but very rarely used, apparently on the theory that they might be construed as limiting the claims to the particular form of the invention shown in the drawing. Reference numerals are often included in the claims of German and certain other foreign patents.

RE-FILE Term not recognized in patent practice. Usually means a *continuation.*

REGISTRATION TO PRACTICE Official admission to practice before the Patent Office, i.e., permission to prepare and *prosecute* applications for patents for others generally, for a fee. Registration is by examination. Examination is waived for applicants who have served 4 or more years in the Examining Corps of the Patent Office. There are about 8000 registrants (practitioners), i.e., patent attorneys and agents. A directory is sold by the Supt. of Documents, Government Printing Office. See *ethics.* Each registrant is assigned a *registration number,* which is usually given on each document that he or she files in the Office. The list of registrants (actually a collection of punch cards) is maintained by the Committee on Enrollment in the Office.

REISSUE Of an application, one that reads the same as an issued patent of the same ownership except for changes made to correct some deficiency or error in the original patent. The purpose of a reissue application is to repair some defect found in the original patent after it was issued. The reissue application must contain an offer to surrender the original patent when the reissue application issues. The resulting *reissue patent* will run only for the unexpired remainder of the term of the original. Reissue patents are numbered in a separate series, e.g., *Re. 12,345.* They number about 0.5 percent of the total number of all U.S. patents. The rules and practice in reissue cases are complex, and changing.

REJECT   By an Examiner, to rule that one or more *claims* in an application are denied, officially considered unpatentable. Only *claims* can be *rejected.* The bulk of an Examiner's work is writing rejections, and these constitute the main issues at stake in the *prosecution* of an *application.* No other word is used in *Office actions* to mean this, and this term is never applied to anything else. In particular, the term *disallow* is not in the vocabulary of patent practice.

REJECTION   1. Act of rejecting a *claim(s).* 2. Office action or letter rejecting claim(s). Claims are said to be *under rejection,* or to *stand rejected.*

It is generally considered desirable to have some, but not all, of the claims submitted in a new application rejected by the Examiner on the first *action.* If all the claims were *allowed* on the first action, it would suggest that the claims were not *broad* enough; it is too late to change them, and one will never know what broader claims might have been allowed, could only they have been submitted. Contrariwise, an application should have some claims specific enough to be allowable on the first action if judgment is correct; the traditional desideratum is a *well-graded set of claims.*

REJECTION, FINAL   An Office *action* rejecting claims, normally for the second time on the same grounds, and stating at the end, "This action is made *final*" — meaning that the Examiner will not reconsider the claims nor admit any further amendments as a matter of the applicant's right. If circumstances warrant, the Examiner *may* enter another amendment, or he may refuse to; he will grant an interview with the object of putting together an amendment that might salvage something in a case that appears to him to have something patentable in it. But the applicant's only right is to appeal from the final rejection to the Board of Appeals. Normally, a final action is the second action in a case. Formerly it was the third action. The easiest, and perhaps usual, *response* to a final rejection when some claims *stand allowed* and there are no serious disagreements between the applicant and the Examiner, is simply to file an *amendment* cancelling all the rejected claims (and complying with any *formal* requirements standing). The case will then routinely go to issue as a patent containing all the claims that were allowed. Actual practice often becomes complicated. See *amendment.*

REMARKS   In an *amendment,* the heading of the section devoted to summarizing the current situation in the prosecution of the case, and to explanation and argument. It is always the last section, and often the longest. If the occasion requires, the *Remarks* will present a detailed analysis of the differences between the *references cited* by the Examiner and the applicant's invention, with a discussion showing in detail what words in the claims in question are believed to distinguish patentably over the references, and why. Three to six pages of Remarks is not unusual.

RES JUDICATA (law)   A thing already decided or adjudged, hence, not to be brought up again. In Office practice, applicable only in certain situations in interferences and appeals. As a general principle in all proceedings, however, no issue, once decided, is to be brought up again. (It's the only way to bring the case to a finish.)

RESPONSE   What an applicant must send back after receiving an Office *letter* or *action,* and within the time limit set. By the Rules, a *response* must answer every *rejection* and *objection* set forth in the *action,* by, e.g., cancellation and/or amendment of claims, correction as required, and appropriate explanation and argument. It is normally in the form of an *amendment.* If it leaves out something required, the Examiner may hold it to be *non-responsive,* and refuse to *enter* it — a hazard to be taken seriously, since it may lead to a holding of *abandonment.* See *amendment, period, timely.* Writing *responses* is perhaps about half of the work done by a patent attorney or agent in the *prosecution* of a case.

RESTRICTION   Cancellation of one or more groups of claims in an application in response to a *requirement for restriction* by an *Examiner,* and filing of other applications, later, containing the cancelled claims. Requirements for restriction are made when the Examiner rules that there are claims directed to more than one separate and *distinct* invention. Only one invention may be claimed in one application. In practice, the usage is complex. Where the claims are of the genus-species type, three species are permitted if a generic claim is allowed, but only one species if it is not. Where the claims are directed to a process or method, the necessary apparatus, and the product, restriction may be required, depending on the official *classifications* of the processes, apparatus, and products concerned.

In genus-species situations, a provisional *election* of species can be made on the premise that the generic claims or claim are not allowable; if they later are allowed, the other species claims may come out of abeyance. A requirement for restriction may be *traversed* by the applicant; the Examiner then may either withdraw it or *make it final* (withdrawal seems to be unusual). Acquiescense in a requirement is accomplished by cancelling or electing the appropriate claims. A *petition* may be taken to the Commissioner from a final requirement. See *election, division, petition.*

RULES OF PRACTICE Set of rules promulgated by Commissioners of Patents over the past century or more under authority of the Patent Statutes, governing the conduct of business in and with the Office. Probably as well established as the statutes; but all must be consistent with them. Embodied since 1975 in Title 37, Code of Federal Regulations, Government Printing Office, about $350. See *Laws,* **MPEP,** *CODE.*

SAID (law) The item previously mentioned in this document (or section or claim, etc.) and no other. Widely used in *claims* for exactness. See *antecedent, claim.*

SCOPE Breadth of coverage, area or totality of subject matter as defined in a claim or claims. Said only of claims. Old stock sentence:
This invention is limited only by the *scope* of its appended claims.
The less detailed or *limited* or *specific* a claim is, the broader its *scope.*

SEARCH There are several kinds: *Preliminary, Infringement, State-of-Art,* and *Validity,* which see. The last three are used bv manufacturing firms.

SEARCH ROOM, PUBLIC A large library-like facility in the Patent and Trademark Office building, Crystal Plaza, Arlington, Virginia, having the only classified set of U.S. patents in the world except the Office examining groups upstairs and, possibly, the International Patent Library in The Hague, Netherlands (of which the U.S. is not a member). In the Public Search Room, a searcher consults the *Manual of Classification,* finds which subclasses to search in, goes to the stacks, takes out the appropriate piles of patents, and scans through them at one of the special tables provided with trough-like fitments to facilitate flipping through the *hard copies.* Help is available for the inexperienced. The room is usually crowded during business hours. Some of the wealthier industrial countries, e.g., West Germany, maintain classified patent collections in several major cities for the convenience of searchers. The U.S.A., however, is able to afford only the one. Twelve public libraries in the U.S. have full sets of U.S. patents in bound volumes in numerical order. Not being classified by subject, these are poor material for searching. See *preliminary search, manual of classification, publication.*

SECRECY 1. State of pending applications. Rule 14: ". . . pending applications are preserved in secrecy. No information will be given by the Office respecting the filing by any particular person of an application . . . nor will access be given . . . without written authority in that particular application from the applicant or his assignee or attorney or agent of record . . . " See full text of Rule 14 in the *Rules of Practice.* After an application has issued as a patent, the file becomes open to the public. See *patented file.* 2. An order applied to applications whose issue as patents is officially judged to be potentially detrimental to the national defense, etc. See *secrecy orders,* Sec. 5.1-5.8 in the *Rules of Practice.*

SENIOR PARTY In an *interference,* the party who filed his application earlier than the *junior party.*

SERIAL NUMBER Number assigned to every new application by the Patent Office, and the primary identification of the case. A new series of numbers is started every five years; hence the filing date as well as the serial no. are required for a definitive identification. In practice, applicants provide more complete data. Abbr. *S.N.* See *identification.*

SET FORTH   To state or describe, in the sense of writing down a piece of new information, particularly with reference to *claims.* Ex.,as might be used in *Remarks:* "Claim 3 *sets forth* the novel shape of the cam in combination with the gear train. . ." Syn. *recite.*

SHIFTING GROUND (law)   A tactic not permitted during the *prosecution* of an application. An Examiner may not, e.g., reject a claim on ground A, then later reject it on another ground B, without good reason. Nor may an applicant argue the patentability of claims on one ground, then switch to another, nor present claims directed all to one aspect of the disclosure and then replace them with claims on a different aspect. Shifting ground fails to *advance the prosecution.*

SHOE (colloq.)   In the Examining Groups of the Office, one of the drawers of the files of *prior art* used for searching. Holds about a 2-inch load of *hard copies,* etc., piled flat. In use, the shoe is removed from the *shoe case* (a tall cabinet), and propped up at an angle.

SHOULD   When used in an *action,* as, "Applicant should . . .," it generally means *had better.*

SKILLED IN THE ART   Having the knowledge of an average working specialist in a subject *(art),* e.g., a polymer chemist; a mechanical engineer specializing in heat transfer; an electronic engineer who professionally designs high-power amplifiers; a professional bookbinder; a skilled machinist. Under 35 U.S.C. 103, an invention, to be patentable, must not "have been *obvious* at the time the invention was made to a person having ordinary skill in the art to which (its subject matter) pertains." See *obvious.*

SOLICITOR   High-level Office employee, working under the Office of the Solicitor, a lawyer with primary duties of representing the Commissioner in appeals to courts, etc. Also concerned with enforcement of ethical conduct among registered attorneys and agents.

SPECIAL   Status of an application which has been authorized to be taken up out of turn, ahead of the backlog or waiting list. Amended cases are *special* compared to new applications. The backlog tends to be roughly of the order of a year long. An applicant can file a *petition to make special,* currently on any of the following grounds:
1. Inventor over 65 years old, or in fragile health.
2. Prospective manufacture of the invention (supporting financial data required).
3. Infringement believed in progress. (Supporting and specific data required.)
4. Invention of a nature to "materially enhance the quality of the environment . . ."
5. Invention related to production or conservation of energy.

Published statistics indicate that such petitions are probably filed in less than 1 percent of applications. Business considerations may not favor the early issuance of a patent, e.g., the time required to build up a market for the product. See *delay.*

SPECIFIC   Of a claim, relatively narrow, detailed, limited. The opposite of *broad.* Does not connote unnecessary narrowness. Often used in the *Remarks* section of *amendments* as a descriptive term suggesting that a claim is allowable.

SPECIFY   A term generally avoided. A *claim* or a *specification* may describe, show, *recite,* say, *set forth,* or state something, but it is not said to specify it.

SOPHISTICATED   In the current technological sense, a term to be avoided as indefinite jargon.

SPECIFICATION   The descriptive part of an application or patent, usually taking up most of the text. The term is sometimes used to mean both the specification and the claims. See *application, claim.* The recommended order for a specification is:
Abstract

> Background of the invention (see *Prior Art statement)*
> Brief summary of invention (without ref. to drawing)
> Short descriptions of Figures of drawing
> Detailed description of invention.

In a complete application, the claims follow, then as the last page, the petition, power of attorney, and declaration or oath form. Formerly, a section giving the "Objects of the Invention" was widely used; but a trend appears to have developed over some decades of writing too many "Objects," and the Office dropped this section from its recommendations. Specification is singular, not plural.

STATE OF THE ART   The whole body of current knowledge generally available to a typical skilled practitioner of an *art,* e.g., all the published or generally known relevant technical information available to a structural engineer, a chemist, a carpenter, etc. A patentable invention must make an advance beyond the *state of the art.* . In engineering literature the expression connotes up-to-dateness, the latest thing. In patent practice, it connotes stuff that is already *old.* See *old.*

STATE-OF-ART SEARCH   A search made to find detailed background information on a specific subject on which, e.g., inventive or development work is planned. Unlike an ordinary library search, it can turn up practical industrial data in highly specialized fields, e.g., the design of oil well tools or the composition of erasing fluids. May typically deliver twenty or thirty patents.

STATUS   Of an application, the current stage in its *prosecution,* e.g., awaiting the first *action;* under rejection (awaiting response from applicant); allowed; on appeal. A *status letter* from an applicant about his case will be mailed back with the status noted on the bottom. Status letters are typically written when it appears that an *action* or other communication from the Office may be overdue, and concern is mounting that something may have got lost somewhere. It is unknown what to do when a status letter appears to have been lost.

STATUTORY BAR   An absolute bar by statute against patenting any invention that has been described in any printed publication or been in public use or on sale more than one year prior to the filing of an application for patent on that invention. 35 U.S.C. 102. See *public use, publication.* Most foreign countries do not even permit the one year's "grace." There is no appeal from a statutory bar.

STATUTORY SUBJECT MATTER   See *invention.*

SUBJECT MATTER   In *claims,* the significant substance of what is written, considered separately from the way in which it is worded. Office *actions* sometimes say that a claim, e.g., "appears to be directed to allowable subject matter;" it means that the claim will be allowed if the language is suitably repaired, as by overcoming some *formal objection* standing against it.

SUBSTANCE   The evident meaning of something, particularly a *claim,* as contrasted with its *form.* An Office *action* may say that a certain claim is allowable in substance; it means the same as in the example given above under *subject-matter.*

SUBSTANTIAL, SUBSTANTIALLY   Enough to matter; enough to make a significant difference; enough to get the effect indicated. Term widely used, particularly in *claims.*

SUCH   Of this general kind; of the sort just mentioned or under discussion. Useful in a specification. Generally avoided in claims as *indefinite.*

SUITABLE   Of a kind or nature appropriate to some stated purpose, taken from the *prior art* and not considered part of the invention. Often used in *specifications.* Ex.:
> The cover may be attached by means of any *suitable* fasteners.
See *according to the invention, known.*

TEACH   To show or disclose something, usually said of a *reference.* An *action* may say, e.g., "The _____ patent *teaches* applicant's combination. See Fig. _____ "

TEACH AWAY Said of a *reference,* to lead the reader away from the inventive concept in an application, as by indicating that a thing of that sort would not work. Not uncommonly, a *cited* reference shows something that superficially resembles a later invention, but turns out on closer inspection to be based on a distinctly different principle. After spotting this, a patent *practitioner* will hunt for some tell-tale passage in the reference that *teaches away* from the invention in his case, for use in overcoming *rejections.*

TECHNOLOGY The term *art* is usually used instead.

TERM The life of a patent, during which its owner has the power to sue infringers. After its *term* has expired, a patent becomes merely a part of the general published technical literature; as such, it is good forever as a *reference* against later patent applications. The term of a U.S. patent is 17 years from the date it is issued. It cannot be extended except by special act of Congress. In some foreign countries, the term of a patent is 20 years from the date of filing the application, and in others, 14 years from the date of issue.
The term of a copyright is 28 years, extendable at the owner's request for another 28 years. Some inventions have been far ahead of the supporting technology, and so cannot profit the inventor or owner until long after any 17-year term. A classic set of cases is the sound-on-film motion picture patents of Clyde Fritts, whose applications were first filed in the 1880's, but could not have been practiced commercially before the mid-1920's.

THEREIN (law) In the particular document, patent, claim, etc. under discussion, and nowhere else.

THERETO (law) A synonym for *to it,* considered more unambiguous.

TIME FOR, TIMELY In the Rules of Practice, MPEP, etc., a designation of a deadline for filing some document, such as a *response,* a Notice of Appeal, or an Appeal Brief. *Timely filed* means filed in time. When a paper is not timely filed, the most common consequence is a holding of *abandonment.* See *abandon.*

TRADEMARK Although the U.S. Patent and Trademark registers trademarks as well as issuing patents, trademark practice is a specialized branch of law quite different from patent practice. For example, a trademark must be actually used in interstate commerce *before* an application for Federal registration can be filed. State laws give some protection to trademarks under the doctrines of unfair competition, apart from any Federal registration. On trademark questions, see an attorney who is registered for trademark practice with the Patent and Trademark Office. To get a preliminary idea whether a proposed trademark has been registered before by somebody else, it is possible to consult a book, "The Trademark Register", found in large public libraries. This commercially-published directory, about the size of a phone book, lists alphabetically all the trademarks in force, giving the registration number of each. Copies of trademarks of interest can be ordered by number from "Commissioner of Patents and Trademarks, Washington, D.C. 20231", for twenty cents each.

TRAILER CLAUSE (law) In an employment agreement, such as is commonly required by U.S. corporations of hired engineers, scientists, and other white-collar workers, a clause assigning to the employer all inventions, or all inventions in some stated category, made by the employee for a stated period of time after he has resigned or been fired. Such clauses have been held by courts to be enforceable for periods of up to 5 years, but not for longer. Trailer clauses are said by some writers to have the effect of making the worker unemployable for the period of the clause in his main field of skill. A current variant is the case of engineer Martin Alter, whose employer obtained a temporary court injunction against his getting a job with a competing corporation on the ground that he might disclose trade secrets.

TRAVERSE By an *applicant,* to formally disagree with an examiner's requirement for *division* or *restriction.* The pertinent *amendment* would state that the requirement was "respectfully traversed," and under *Remarks* would explain the reasons, which are apt to be rather technical. See *restriction.*

TREATY   See *Patent Cooperation Treaty.*

UNOBVIOUS   A key word in a key section of the statutes, 35 U.S.C. 103. An invention, to be patentable, must be both new and unobvious. See *invention, obvious, skilled in the art.*

UP TO   In the sense of setting forth the degree of some quantity, as, "pressures up to 3000 psi," avoided as being *indefinite;* reserved to the popular media. The expressions "no greater than," "no less than" are, however, OK. See *as much as.*

U.S.C.   United States Code. Title 35 (*cited* as 35 U.S.C.) contains most of the Federal statutes on patents, trademarks, and copyrights. See *Laws,* "35 U.S.C. 102" means section 102 of Title 35, U.S. Code.

VAGUE   A common ground of *rejection* of *claims,* usually stated as *vague and indefinite.* Based on the statute 35 U.S.C. 112, which requires a patent *specification* to be "full, concise and exact" and the claims to "particularly point out and distinctly claim" the invention. See *alternative, claim, ground of rejection, indefinite, inference.*

VALIDITY   Of a patent, or a *claim* or claims in a patent, the quality of being enforceable against infringers. Validity is outside the powers of the Patent and Trademark Office, being under the jurisdiction of the Federal courts. Patents, their applications having been examined and, as it were, filtered by the Office, have a legal presumption of validity. How strong the presumption is, is a matter of learned dispute. Federal courts in infringement suits, often hold some or all of the *claims* of a patent *invalid.* The percentage of patents held invalid in decisions of Federal Circuit Courts of Appeal varies from an average of about 50 percent to about 92 percent, depending on the circuit. Against this somewhat disturbing background, one experienced patent attorney has observed that a well-prepared patent on an invention of clear originality and merit is, allegedly, likely to be upheld in court, and that it is mostly the doubtful patents that get litigated — in accord with the old principle that a lawsuit is unlikely unless each party thinks he has a fair chance of winning.

VALIDITY SEARCH   An extra-thorough search for prior art in the Public Search Room and elsewhere, by attorneys acting for a defendant or prospective defendant in an infringement suit. The object is to find some *art* that might defeat the patent concerned, art closer than was found by the Examiner during the prosecution of the application for the patent and shown in the *patented file.* The attorneys also may pay several hundred dollars for a search in the International Patent Library in the Hague, which is generally considered better than any such facility in the U.S. A validity search may consume several man-weeks or months of time, and is expensive, and occurs mainly in connection with larger corporate lawsuits.

WHEREBY   As a result of which. Often used in *claims* as the first word of a final clause (a "whereby" clause) which *sets forth* the result of the operation of the preceding elements, to tie the claim together. Ex.:

> A mouse trap comprising:
> · · · · · ,
> · · · · · ,
> · · · · · , and
> · · · · · ,
> whereby the mouse is caught.

WHEREIN (law)   In which.

WORK   1. Of a patent, to use it commercially, by manufacturing and selling the patented article, or by commercially using the patented process. In many foreign countries, a patent must be *worked* in order for it to continue in force. 2. A blank or semi-finished object worked on by a tool or a machine; a workpiece.

WORLD INTELLECTUAL PROPERTY ORGANIZATION (WIPO)   An office in Geneva, Switzerland, which administers various international treaties relating to patents, trademarks, and copyrights and does certain collateral work such as gathering statistics and publishing the journal *Industrial Property*. Supported jointly by the member countries, which are practically all the industrial nations. WIPO was established in the late 1960's to replace the much older *BIRPI* on a gradual basis. Both are located side by side in office buildings in Geneva. Its chief responsibilities at present are the administration of the new *Patent Cooperation Treaty* and the *European Patent Convention*.